CENSORSHIP AND FREE SPEECH

Censorship and Free Speech

Some Philosophical Bearings

P.G. INGRAM
The Queen's University of Belfast

Routledge
Taylor & Francis Group
LONDON AND NEW YORK

First published 2000 by Ashgate Publishing

Reissued 2019 by Routledge
2 Park Square, Milton Park, Abingdon, Oxon, OX14 4RN
52 Vanderbilt Avenue, New York, NY 10017

Routledge is an imprint of the Taylor & Francis Group, an informa business

A Library of Congress record exists under LC control number:

ISBN 13: 978-1-138-73478-4 (hbk)
ISBN 13: 978-1-315-18702-0 (ebk)

Contents

Series Preface

The objective of the Dartmouth Series in Applied Legal Philosophy is to publish work which adopts a theoretical approach to the study of particular areas or aspects of law or deals with general theories of law in a way which focuses on issues of practical moral and political concern in specific legal contexts.

In recent years there has been an encouraging tendency for legal philosophers to utilize detailed knowledge of the substance and practicalities of law and a noteworthy development in the theoretical sophistication of much legal research. The series seeks to encourage these trends and to make available studies in law which are both genuinely philosophical in approach and at the same time based on appropriate legal knowledge and directed towards issues in the criticism and reform of actual laws and legal systems.

The series will include studies of all the main areas of law, presented in a manner which relates to the concerns of specialist legal academics and practitioners. Each book makes an original contribution to an area of legal study while being comprehensible to those engaged in a wide variety of disciplines. Their legal content is principally Anglo-American, but a wide-ranging comparative approach is encouraged and authors are drawn from a variety of jurisdictions.

TOM D. CAMPBELL
Series Editor
The Faculty of Law
The Australian National University

Preface

The very use of the term 'censorship' today often suggests that the activity denoted is one for disapproval. There may be a widespread belief—in western countries, certainly—that anyone who reflects deeply about this activity has no option but to conclude that, whatever its purpose, it is intrinsically reprehensible. If there has been almost universal acceptance that it is, with the result that 'to praise an act of censorship is to verge on committing a linguistic mistake',[1] we should realize that it is more than an assumption which should not be taken for granted. I make no attempt to prove or disprove the reprehensibility of censorship in what I have written in the following pages. All that I ask of my readers is that for the sake of the discussion they should accept my use of the word 'censorship' as far as possible as the use of a neutrally descriptive term, referring to more than those restrictions on freedom of expression of which we disapprove and which we therefore unhesitatingly call by their proper name.

I should make it clear that while I do not take for granted that censorship is wrong, equally what I have written is in no way intended as an apology for censorship, although certain passages might suggest the contrary. In this work I have not attempted any sustained empirical treatment of the practice of censorship either in the past or at the present time. Accordingly, few references will be found to actual cases of censorship. Some readers may criticize these omissions as leaving my arguments divorced from reality and claim that a careful assessment of censorship in practice could hardly have allowed me to put forward in some places so impassive a view of deliberate restraints on individual freedom. To my mind the truth of the matter is perhaps that the practice of censorship is bound up with other considerations which may distract both those who give it effect and those who are subjected to it from seeing either the basic structure and aims of censorship itself or indeed the less than beneficial character of some uses of free speech. Through references to actual examples the reader might have been distracted from central philosophical concerns by the ideological overtones of a particular case, the unacceptability of the methods used or confusion over the results intended—and even by partisan feelings. With a few exceptions I have tried to keep my references to censorship non-specific; and in all cases I have simplified examples beyond what might conceivably be found existing in the real world. Censorship as an issue of principle can only be considered fairly in an abstracted form. The accretions of practice have often only a contingent relation to the restrictions involved, and they may mislead people concerned about principles into unprofitable diversions.

What then have I sought to do? The brief work that follows is in no sense a fully comprehensive study of the restriction of freedom of expression and information, even in the abstract. The attempt I have made is to offer a selective view of the relation of censorship and free speech to the individual and society. The introductory chapter is developed to indicate what is properly covered by the term 'censorship'. A simple statement of a definition would hardly be satisfactory: the different varieties of censorship must be made clear, and, most importantly, it must be shown that these varieties are related in a significant way. The aim of the first chapter is therefore to counter the sort of argument which would treat instances of censorship type by type, and area by area, seeing them not just as superficially different but as fundamentally distinct. The other aim of this chapter is to get away from a preoccupation with pornography and obscenity. These are topics which often seem to dominate discussions of censorship at the present time, but arguably they may not be socially very important. Indeed, our concern with sexual obscenity does not appear to have been a preoccupation of all, or even most, past civilizations. Therefore they ought not to be seen as the central point of reference for arguments about freedom of speech.

Following clarification of a concept of censorship the discussion may move on to more fruitful topics. The aim of devoting a section of the second chapter to the treatment of some common criticisms of censorship is not only to refute them or modify them severely, but also to attempt to redress—to a degree—the emotive balance in our responses to censorship and to introduce some of those themes that will recur in later sections. The rest of the book needs no explanation here. If in the third chapter I seem close to establishing an unassailable, privileged position for the individual's freedom of speech, this is only to make the dilemma posed by the status of free speech in society a starker one. In the final chapter I put forward some of the limits on free speech that follow on practical constraints; these cannot be eliminated or even properly compensated for. To conclude I state some of the limits that follow on theoretical constraints;

these may ostensibly be a matter of philosophical choice, but to what extent can they really be so?

I offer no solution to the problem of the proper extent of censorship in a society. In the end such a solution cannot be derived deductively from a philosophical study of free speech; rather it must depend on the position adopted regarding a much greater question, namely about the nature of a society and the individual's place in it. If I have made any kind of original contribution to this problem I would hope that it is in showing that censorship and, more widely, other restrictions on freedom cannot be considered in a self-contained way but have implications of which the advocate of unrestricted freedom for the individual in matters of opinion seems surprisingly unaware. To adopt a position on censorship is not merely to say something about the rights of individuals or the proper role of the state or other authorities: it is also to make a statement about a proper conception of society and the social existence of its members.

Note

1 Frederick Schauer, 'The Ontology of Censorship', in Robert C. Post (ed.), *Censorship and Silencing: Practices of Cultural Regulation* (Los Angeles, 1998), p. 147.

1 Preliminaries

A Definition of Censorship

What is censorship? Initially, the answer to this question may appear so straightforward as hardly to be worth answering. A more difficult question is: what amounts to censorship? It is the significance and consequences of actions which have a censoring effect as well as the express practice of censorship, with which I shall be concerned in the following pages.

For many people—including, I imagine, the reader who has just opened this book—the word 'censorship' immediately suggests an activity to be condemned. Yet I think that if we allow ourselves unprejudicially to reflect on what may be referred to by the use of that word we will become aware of a complex of different social, political and moral problems meriting a range of restrictive responses which can be motivated and justified in not a few distinct ways. According to the case in question, restrictions on free speech may be seen as beneficial rather than detrimental, as necessary and desirable for society and not just expedient for the state or the government. Final judgments on censorship in general (if a single unequivocal conclusion is ever possible) as well as our opinions about censorship in particular cases will be dependent on the relative weights which we allot to diverse social values. In this book I aim to relate the value of free speech either directly to other values or to the social activities in which those values are embodied. By doing so I intend to provide a way of reassessing the place of public restrictions on freedom of expression.

Despite the complexities of what can be considered to amount in actuality to censorship, the best way to begin is with a definition of the explicit practice, since in discussion the term 'censorship' can be used in a wide-ranging manner that is not well-considered or substantiated. Censorship has been around for a long time, and so as a starting-point I take a sixty-year-old definition of the term which is clear and by no means out of date: censorship is 'the policy of restricting the public expression of ideas, opinions, conceptions and impulses which have or are believed to have the capacity to undermine the governing authority or the social and moral order which that authority considers itself bound to protect'.[1] I will come to modify this definition in some of my arguments in the following pages, but, taken as it stands for a starting-point, it requires some comments.

Firstly, censorship is claimed to be a policy of restriction: it is typically the policy of restricting the public expression of ideas. Two points immediately arise. First, that there is a policy involved implies that the practice is to a degree regular and rule-guided and, in addition, that it serves some external purpose, such as a moral principle or a political strategy. What the wider purpose of censorship may be is a theme which runs through this book. (At the same time, it should be borne in mind that censorship may in fact be practised in an irregular, arbitrary and self-defeating fashion.) Second, that censorship is about restriction highlights its connection with intolerance. It is not difficult to see that a desire to restrict involves a measure of intolerance. However, it is instructive to note how censorship and intolerance differ. Intolerance seeks to suppress completely, and not only to suppress expression but the thoughts themselves which give rise to that expression. Although censorship may on occasion bring about a total suppression of some ideas, more often than not it does not place an absolute ban on the expression of ideas but requires alterations or omissions within that expression, changes in detail, deletion of some content, or its confinement to a certain class of audience. Although censorship may result in suppression in particular cases, it typically and centrally involves restriction rather than suppression. It is not concerned so much to suppress the expression of an opinion as to effect changes within it or limit its dissemination in order that what is expressed falls within the limits of what received opinion or government itself wishes to permit. Of course, a government which imposes such restrictions as a policy intends that there should be further effects. I shall discuss some consequences of successsful restrictions at a later point in connection with the substantive links that exist between freedom of expression and freedom of thought; as I shall show, these two freedoms are inseparable in the real world.

Secondly, censorship is concerned with publication, or public performance or exhibition. It is the practice of restricting the public expression of ideas. It is directed towards the expression influenced by those thoughts. By contrast, intolerance is concerned with a person's ideas and thoughts in their own right. When a movement becomes the victim of intolerance it is suppressed; its members are often subjected to penal sanctions on account of the content of their beliefs, whether or not those beliefs are deliberately publicized or otherwise made known to the general public. Censorship attends to public expression. When it seems to interfere with opinions held privately only, it is perhaps seeking to anticipate and prevent their public expression. It is not typically concerned with privately held opinions or knowledge for their own sake; it is directed towards, and with respect to, their public dissemination.

In these introductory remarks about the definition of censorship it is appropriate to make some comments about the relation of censorship to free speech. Much censorship frequently only changes or edits the expression of ideas and opinions; therefore the existence of a policy of censorship does not of itself mean the complete control of people's public opinions—the total absence of freedom—but rather the limitation or qualification of their freedom of expression. Let us accept from the start that no matter how extensive free speech is in any society it is always at some points limited or qualified. However liberal our attitudes we do not think that the complete absence of what we willingly call censorship would bring about a freedom of speech that was completely unchecked. Free speech will always have its bounds. The classical examples are familiar enough: a man cannot wantonly shout 'Fire!' in a crowded theatre when there is nothing amiss, or publish abusive and untruthful statements about personal enemies, or (undesirably not only from the authorities' point of view but also for ordinary citizens going about their everyday business) incite an angry mob with revolutionary statements in support of violence, or—to suggest more contemporary examples—make hoax bomb warnings or advocate paedophilia. Our liberal beliefs are safeguarded, it seems, because we readily believe that an abuse of free speech is in some significant, if paradoxical, sense not an example of free speech at all; consequently, the restriction of such abuse does not amount to censorship. But this begs the question of what is to count as an abuse of free speech. To imply, if not to say explicitly, that universally acceptable restrictions do not amount to censorship is unhelpful in coming to terms with the point of restricting what people say and write and publish. It also makes it difficult to accept that boundaries shift between accepted and unaccepted expression and acceptable and unacceptable restrictions, and to understand how they do.

Freedom of information, like freedom of expression, is similarly bound to be limited. Although there may be criticisms concerning their abuse, the necessity of some restrictions on public information in the interests of national security is not disputed. A society must always protect itself against immediate threats to public order, its stability and its own existence. In pursuit of these ends limitations on many kinds of freedoms are almost universally thought justified; foreclosing public access to sensitive factual information (particularly of a military or economic kind) is at least a necessary evil. In appropriate circumstances measures of censorship may be provided with analogous justifications to those based on national security. Reference may be made to a short-term need to maintain public order or social stability or a longer-term need to defend society against internal threats, as, for example, in the areas of race relations or the prevention of terrorism, rather than immediate dangers. Debate in these areas concerns the extent of restrictions, not the principle of restriction itself.

Certainly we may still continue to think of censorship in general as undesirable; we may even believe it to be an evil to be avoided altogether in all but the most exceptional circumstances. However, it is not correct to assume that censorship leads inexorably to a general destruction of liberty or that it is by its very nature a repressive social or legal activity. To limit the abuse of a freedom is not repression. Therefore not all restriction is repression, and censorship is only one limitation of liberty among many in every democratic society. Censorship needs examination of an impartial kind, as a term covering certain restrictive activities which will at a minimum sometimes be justifiable in their motivations and aims and beneficial in their consequences for the majority of society's members. Of course, it may still be argued that freedom of speech is a paramount value, outweighing any social disadvantages and even harm that can rightly be attributed to it in a particular instance; but the discussion of this position is more properly left for me to take up later.

Forms and Methods

At the beginning of this book I posed the question: 'what amounts to censorship?' Although it may seem premature for me to indulge so early in an excursus on the forms taken by explicit censorship and the methods used to enforce censorship both directly and indirectly, I am doing this in order to show that although wide and rather vague references to 'censorship' may sometimes be mistaken, the extent of restrictions amounting to censorship is much greater than the few activities clearly covered by the ordinary use of the term. My contention here is that as far as issues of principle are concerned, direct and indirect censorship are to be considered together. Censorship is to be assessed in relation to its motivation and intentions rather than its means. It should also be seen that to describe censorship as a policy—a word which suggests deliberate and well-defined intentions—is often to mischaracterize it. Censorship of an indirect kind may sometimes be haphazard, and often the policies and principles behind it (whatever they are) are not capable of being easily or clearly formulated.

The most obvious form of censorship is the legal form. Censorship of this kind may be well formulated in clear laws which define its purpose and scope, those officials who have power to enforce the laws, and the ways in which they are to be enforced; or it may be couched in very general terms imposing few strict limits, as with the Official Secrets Acts in the United Kingdom, which can, if required, be construed to cover a vast range of cases; or it may be vaguer still, giving wide discretionary powers to officials of many kinds to impose restrictions as they see fit.[2]

Legal measures may amount to full or partial censorship. The latter is exemplified by the 'adults only' tag on some magazines and films; but it is not necessarily confined to the distinction between child and adult. Partial censorship can be practised, for example, through distinctions based on class, education, or purpose. A partial censorship that we so often do not question is with us all the time in the distinction between information accessible only to public officials and information accessible to the general public. From time to time there is talk of 'open government', but however genuinely open our government may be, there will always be a large amount of factual information, policy considerations and comment which are excluded from the public domain but to which the public arguably have a right of access.[3]

A quite different area of selective censorship is provided by the way in which in the past certain books have been published solely in an expensive edition; the denial of easy availability for suspect material has from time to time been used as a crude measure to ensure that they would not be read by the 'wrong' people. This has not been the case only with pornography; with revolution so much in the air in the last decade of the eighteenth century one famous objection to Thomas Paine's *Rights of Man* was that it was published at such a low price as to find a wide distribution among the lower classes; and since newspapers and periodicals percolated to those classes at the time they were prone to encounter serious restrictions. Expensive books could be relied on not to fall into the wrong hands without the need for formal restrictive measures. Further examples of selective censorship at the present time are found in the ways sensitive material—books, videos and the like of a sexual or violent nature—may be readily available to people like doctors and lawyers for their professional purposes but not to the general public whose interest in the material could presumably only be prurient. Full censorship entails a universal application of the measures involved, without regard to distinctions between classes or groups of individuals. No censorship is ever completely universal, of course, since someone must always see the material in order to censor it or continue the restrictions; and, short of the physical destruction of uncensored material, such material remains available to certain persons in virtue of their office. Nevertheless, it is worth while to maintain a pragmatic distinction in place between partial and full censorship.

Related to legal censorship are a number of different kinds which may broadly be included under the term 'quasi-legal'. The clearest examples are found in actions taken by those in some official capacity who nevertheless have no express legal backing for what they do in the case in question. In the United Kingdom successive governments have used various means (in particular, the so-called D-notices) to 'advise' the media that references to certain matters or the publication of certain information would not be in the public interest. Especially in the past, such instructions were usually heeded, although no formal prior sanctions could be legally enforced. Of course, if there are no legal sanctions to be threatened, the success of any measures depends on tacit understandings and agreements. When these can no longer be taken for granted, old systems of restrictions either break down or are transformed into more explicit, legally backed procedures. Other quasi-legal forms of censorship are applied not by governmental authorities but by public bodies and institutions, private employers, professional associations, private clubs and societies, and even political parties. The limitation of a person's freedom of speech may be an actual or effective condition of membership or employment, as evidenced by the use of gagging clauses in contracts and other measures to deter 'whistle-blowing' or render it ineffective. Alternatively, although there may be no pre-existing restrictions in place, the consequences of speaking out are all too clear.

Why do we have so many kinds of both legal and extra-legal censorship in a supposedly free society? Obviously, many restrictions can be linked to the distribution and maintenance of power—by a state over its citizens, by a company over its employees, by a club or political party over its members. Beyond their overt functions they must also be seen in many instances as formalized or organized extensions of social censorship, although this also often reduces either to a manifestation of the desire of a majority to constrain a minority or to the intention of a minority with power and influence to continue to impose on the majority the values in which they believe. Informal social censorship on its own lacks the backing of law or specific authority but has from time to time been no less powerful. It may occasionally take a direct form, as, for example, where a small social group ostracizes offending members, either leading them to mend their ways by encouraging the practice of self-censorship, or denying them effective self-expression. It is much more likely to take indirect forms which discourage the expression of unacceptable opinions or ensure that other members of the community are prevented by social pressures from actively taking up whatever ideas have been disseminated. Social censorship and other restrictions limiting free speech extend importantly into the field of education and the general upbringing of children to ensure that these fall within the range of the usual social expectations. Education is a wide area with its own special problems and I shall be giving this subject more detailed treatment in due course.

In its legal, quasi-legal, and social forms censorship is manifested in two ways, either in penal sanctions following the transgression of a law or in pre-censorship and 'prior restraint', where publication of offending information or opinions is prevented in advance. The former, naturally, is intended to encourage the self-imposition of the latter. Sanctions will mostly be associated with the legal form, through fines, imprisonment, or the destruction of books and other matter, or with the extra-legal form, through loss of employment or other material advantages. Sanctioning measures of a kind can be enforced in connection with more diffuse social desires for censorship, but in a heterogeneous society they will tend to be non-existent or weak because of their informality; in order to be effective, such measures require a strong social cohesion based on common, shared beliefs not only about a basic system of values but also about the detailed interpretation of that system. Whatever our society was like in the past, to say that it lacks a homogeneous character at the present time needs no argument.

Pre-censorship may be of two kinds. The clearest example is where material for publication in any way is submitted for clearance beforehand (as all films and videos for public showing or sale in the United Kingdom are submitted before distribution to the British Board of Film Classification in order to obtain a certificate). Publication will be permitted with or without changes, or with restrictions as to age, or forbidden altogether.[4] If the state or other authority had complete control of the media of publication, pre-censorship would eliminate entirely the need for possibly offensive penal sanctions. If formal pre-censorship is thoroughly effective, it naturally leads to the second, more informal kind, namely voluntary self-censorship; in this case, for example, the writer of a book simply avoids giving information or expressing opinions which he knows will not be allowed to see the light of day. It is this kind of informal pre-censorship that gives real effect to social restrictions, which for the most part lack operative sanctions. It seems plausible to suggest that part of the business of education is to create a ready capacity for this socially necessary self-censorship, which avoids giving offence and, more positively, assists in strengthening the individual's conformity to established social norms, norms that still exist even in a plural society.

Accusations are made that in modern societies the nature of the media (in particular their commercial control) is such as to amount in effect to providing a means for effective censorship. Access to the media is so limited that freedom of expression is seriously affected. Physical constraints on a medium like broadcasting, for example, seem to limit the expression of minority opinions. The problem may be lessened by the introduction of digital broadcasting and other technological developments, and by alternative means of dissemination through the internet, but at present these constraints, in the eyes of some people, create a requirement for conformity. (As circumstances change, of course, the freedom offered by the rapid technological developments of the 1990s are beginning to be seen as a threat, not least by governments.) Accordingly, because of the natural constraints imposed in the allocation and control of finite material resources, people may be led to engage in self-censorship of their own work. Seeking the publication or dissemination of their ideas, and realizing that in their original form they are unlikely to be accepted for publication by reason of their lack of commercial appeal, people may modify what they say and how they say it in order to make it acceptable or popular, thereby—perhaps—doing their ideas and themselves a disservice. True freedom of speech is affected in practice insofar as extrinsic requirements lead to substantive change in content. However, such constraints cannot in general be straightforwardly described as censorship, since it is not necessary for those with control over the media to have a specific intention to bring about such change. Of course, commercial constraints are not inflexible: on the one hand, the choice is often open to overcome them in some way; on the other hand, they are equally open to abuse in order to restrict free speech.

My claim earlier was that the definition of censorship as a policy is not sufficiently broad a term to cover actual censorship in practice, even when areas of supposed censorship such as those mentioned in the foregoing paragraph are excluded. The word 'policy' satisfactorily characterizes most examples of legal censorship as well as many instances of the extra-legal kind. But outside education, where measures of social censorship may be given a kind of formal definition, most social restrictions and sanctions and the intentions and motivations underlying them can hardly be described as resulting from, or being evidence of, or amounting to, a policy or policies. Social censorship is typically informal and unsystematized, and although it will also refer back, in a sometimes half-conscious way, to a system of principled values or beliefs which account for the attitudes that people adopt, it does not involve a consciously thought-out policy, for it will often be given effect on a case-by-case basis. At the worst, it may be no more than a 'knee-jerk' reaction resulting from a passing public concern motivated in part by media coverage.

The word 'policy' is therefore not strictly necessary to a definition of censorship, although the existence of a policy or policies will especially characterize the legal sort, and it is in terms of policies that some of the principles and problems underlying censorship are most profitably and most easily discussed. All that needs to be said is that censorship is the restriction of the public expression of ideas, opinions, and information, insofar as, and because, they are believed to have the capacity to undermine the political, social, or moral order. As well as including official forms of censorship, this brief definition covers the more informal kind of attempted social censorship where little more than forceful disapproval is conveyed because it is felt that the basis of social life is threatened in some way.

Three Aspects of Free Speech

For the sake of convenience the freedom which censorship impairs may generally be referred to as freedom of speech; nevertheless, censorship has three separable aspects which I shall refer to as freedom of expression, freedom of information, and freedom of communication. Any government or other authority can seek to make its policy of censorship effective by attending wholly or chiefly to one of these three aspects. Of course it is unlikely that in practice any policy of censorship will concentrate so completely on one of them alone, but it could do so; and the presence of complete freedom under one aspect alone does not guarantee the existence of a reasonable free speech in general or even a comparative freedom under the other two aspects.

Taken in its literal sense, free speech refers to freedom of expression. In this respect, censorship is practised in many ways, for example by the editing and prohibition of books, by restrictions on radio and television programmes, by the vetting and banning of public speeches, by the removal of exhibits from art exhibitions and by the blocking of access to objectionable websites by internet service providers. Such measures immediately affect freedom of communication as well, but the point to be noted is that, as measures against expression, they concentrate on what is actually said, who is saying it, or how publicly it is being said, rather than on the application of restrictions to the medium through which it is said or the intended recipients. Freedom of expression is in one way the most important aspect of free speech since if it can be satisfactorily controlled, there is little cause to bother about freedom of information and communication; the latter can be left outwardly unimpaired.

Freedom of information is in a way the converse of freedom of expression. It relates to the ability of an interested person to gain access to whatever information it is that he requires. A central example of censorship in this area is the restriction on access to state documents of both present and past importance, a restriction existing to a considerable extent in all countries. However, the extent of freedom of information is also qualified by the ability of the ordinary person generally to read what interests him, have reasonable access to whatever has been published, watch freely television programmes and see films whatever their content, receive radio or satellite broadcasts from a foreign country without being prosecuted for doing so, attend meetings and listen to speakers, whatever their religious beliefs, political opinions or moral attitudes, look at artistic works, or search for information on the internet without hindrance. If there is freedom of expression in a society, then freedom of information—in this wide sense—complements it and, indeed, is necessary to give it meaning. Clearly, an unhindered freedom to speak when nobody was allowed to listen or to publish books that nobody was allowed to distribute for sale would be quite worthless. Conversely, freedom of information would have a limited value in a society where freedom of expression was severely restricted.

Initially, freedom of communication might seem to consist simply in a combination of freedom of expression and freedom of information. Yet the nature of this freedom is more complex. Although measures directly affecting communication are not usually classified under censorship proper, their effect—whether intended or actual—may be exactly the same. The communication of ideas may be hampered by the imposition of taxes in various ways, as sometimes happened in the past with newspapers and magazines, by material restrictions on the media such as control of the allocation of broadcasting frequencies, by interference with the mail and the monitoring of telecommunications, thus practically inhibiting or restricting an individual's ability to express his ideas or gather information without specifically forbidding whatever he is doing or directly interfering with him. Freedom of communication is especially important in two ways: first, facility in the exchange of opinion and information is necessary for the growth of knowledge and the development of ideas; second, it is a reasonable access to the media of communication that determine the real extent of a positive freedom of speech.[5] In any case, free speech must fundamentally be about freedom of communication because the use of language is at its heart a communicative activity and finds much of its value as such.[6]

Conceptually separable though they are, the three aspects of free speech and censorship are obviously intertwined in practice; many measures of direct censorship and other restrictions cannot be confined to one aspect only. The jamming of radio broadcasts and attempts to control and restrict the internet, for example, attack directly and equally the freedoms of expression, information and communication all together. The three aspects are perhaps of minor significance in arguments for and against censorship, which, however it is applied, stands or falls on quite other considerations. But it is as well to differentiate them since, in my discussions of censorship that follow, it occasionally needs to be borne in mind that from time to time measures are directed against free speech under one of the three aspects specifically. The risk is that when restrictive measures appear to leave free speech alone in some ways, they will not be seen as amounting to censorship.

Areas of Restriction

What I have said so far about defining censorship and analysing its methods and forms may imply that censorship can be considered as if it were all of a piece. Up to this point I have made no mention of the evident fact that censorship has separable areas of operation, distinct causes and motivations, and a variety of functions and aims. A minimal censorship of motion pictures, grading them by age, for example, with the simple aim of protecting children from exposure to certain subjects before they are mature enough to cope with the problems raised by them has surely nothing in common with a deliberate policy of forbidding the publication of writings expressing a disfavoured political or social viewpoint, a policy of which numerous examples past and present can be found throughout the world. Nor is it apparent that the banning of a book on the ground that it tends to deprave and corrupt is necessarily connected with its prohibition on the ground, say, that it gives offence to a considerable portion of the population, although such grounds may be closely linked in the public mind.

There are several major areas in which censorship commonly operates. At first sight they appear to be quite separate; but a second look suggests that they may not be merely interconnected but thoroughly enmeshed with one another. I offer five distinct areas for illustration: religion, politics, morals, culture, and (for want of a better term to refer to the world of ideas generally) intellectual matters.

Religious censorship is easily characterized; in its central and most serious instances it is directed towards heresy and blasphemy, and (less intensively perhaps) against the publication and dissemination of heterodox opinions in religious matters. Although this focus of restriction seemed at one time to be disappearing, the demand—at the time of the publication of *The Satanic Verses* by Salman Rushdie in 1988—for the revival of religious censorship through a revision of the blasphemy laws reminds us that religion is ever-present as a potentially restrictive force in society.[7]

Moral censorship is also picked out easily, especially today when among matters of liberty it seems to dominate our concerns about sexual morality and a limited number of other areas: obscenity, pornography, violence and drugs are all current subjects of moral concern, which are often reflected in demands for restrictions on the depiction of these subjects in the wrong light. However, other areas of morality may also be involved; for instance, in its early days the BBC would not permit wicked or criminal individuals to be depicted favourably or the police unfavourably—although a restriction of this kind may be supported by a pragmatic as much as a moral rationale.

Again, political censorship is not difficult to distinguish in central cases; it may be applied to prevent the expression of seditious or subversive opinions, or, more widely and less definitely, it may be applied to prevent or limit the dissemination of opinions of a character not favoured by those in authority. Certainly, in some countries constitutional opposition parties are in no way subversive of the state but, all the same, suffer restrictions and prohibitions; the presumption must be simply that they threaten those in government with the loss of their power. Political censorship, of course, takes not only 'party-political' but also ideological forms.

Cultural expression is another area in which control is exercised in part through censorship. For example, it may be necessary to protect one language and its culture by discriminating against a competing second language or other manifestations of ethnicity—or indeed it may simply be expedient to do so. The use of a state's official language may be promoted by measures restricting or banning public use of other languages; even western democracies provide examples of such policies, with measures restricting the public use of English in France and Quebec.

Finally, intellectual censorship may be the result of measures taken deliberately by a recognized authority, but it may also be the consequence of unorganized pressures originating in society. For example, in an extreme case the crank has no chance at all of getting his book published, although there is no law enjoining all publishers to refuse to publish it. Such pressures may indeed be so informal and indeterminate that they can hardly count as censorship proper at all, yet to the victim the censorship may seem real enough.

Can these different areas of censorship be kept apart? Intellectual censorship may come about through indirect social pressure, or by more direct but not legally grounded measures—major bookselling chains may refuse to stock a certain book and thereby, because of their almost monopolistic position, seriously restrict the writer's freedom of expression. (It is both a merit and demerit of the internet that such restrictions can now be circumvented—a merit because access to knowledge and opinion can no longer be practically restricted, a demerit because there is often no possibility of checking on the quality or veracity of material accessed.) In the past in western countries, restrictive power in intellectual areas was frequently exercised by the political or religious authorities; elsewhere in the world it often still is today. If this happens, it no longer seems plainly to be a matter of intellectual censorship alone, but also one of political or religious censorship, for intellectual ideas are then deemed to fall within the remit of politics or religion. The government may hold that such ideas are politically dangerous or in conflict with the 'authoritative' position—the received opinion—on the same matters; or the clerical authorities may be convinced that an intellectual position threatens religion or is in conflict with the religious dogma of the time. From an opposite point of view, but in a similar way, it is conceivable that the intellectual should wish to suppress certain religious opinions because they seemed to threaten disinterested scientific thought. Some scientists have argued that astrology or homeopathic medicine, for example, should not be treated by the media as if they were on a par with, respectively, astronomy or conventional medicine.[8]

Confusion comes about here not simply because the field of intellectual censorship is less easily or clearly defined than the other three fields. Morals too fall quite often within the remit of religion. The Roman Catholic church has always claimed authority in both faith and morals, and in Islamic countries it can be hard to separate religion, morals and politics, so closely are they intertwined culturally and intellectually. Although the two areas are conceptually separable for many western thinkers, and morality certainly need not depend on religious belief, the association of a moral and a religious system for many people (and not Catholics alone) ensures that the two areas of religion and morality will be closely linked. If certain persons are prepared to acknowledge the right of a church to adjudicate in religious matters, overruling individual conscience, they are also likely to accept its right to interfere in moral matters on what are in the end religious as well as moral grounds. In less formal ways too, questions of religion may be brought to bear on moral arguments; the argument against pornographic literature and its distribution, for example, may be partly based on the idea of 'a Christian society'.

Nor does political censorship stand alone. I have already suggested that intellectual censorship may take place for political reasons and thus also be an example of the political kind, insofar as there is an implied claim that an intellectual position has some political content or significance. Cultural censorship is even more clearly a political concern too. Religion and morality may have political relevance or associations, and events in the former Yugoslavia provide only one sort of example among many of their reality and human cost. Even when the political and cultural associations of religion are, as in Ireland, more historical and formal than substantively related to contemporary styles of everyday living, they still remind us that religion is not as politically moribund everywhere as it seems to be in

England.[9] Regarding the political importance of morality we may note the arguments expressed by Lord Devlin over thirty years ago but still current in the feelings and beliefs of many ordinary people—and politicians too—that the upholding of morality by the law is necessary for the maintenance of society: in other words, a lax or corrupted morality may be as subversive for the structure of a particular society as any ostensibly more political activity.[10]

The conclusion must be drawn not that no act of religious or political censorship ever is only religious or political, for it is unarguable that many acts of religious censorship in the past have had only a religious significance. (In addition, as far as we are concerned, restrictions in the name of morality today have justifying them largely moral reasons and purposes.) Rather, many acts of religious restriction, as is clear from the most cursory reading of history, may be more than religious because they have political significance as well, and some ostensibly religious restrictions may have little intrinsic religious importance at all but are enacted for their intended moral or political effect.

At this point I should mention that I do not choose here or elsewhere to discuss artistic censorship directly. This may have already struck some readers as a strange omission, particularly as artistic merit is often cited as a redeeming feature of some work that might otherwise be deemed obscene on sexual or other grounds. I hold, however, that discussion of artistic censorship is quite naturally subsumed under other headings. The only reason that the world of art and literature might be considered to have an autonomy of its own would be if artistic merit were somehow objectively determinable independent of any context. This, of course, would be impossible. Artistic merit is itself socially and historically determined; how it is defined is consequent on cultural values for us, and in other societies on political and religious factors. The ways in which art and literature are affected by freedoms and restrictions, therefore, is an expression of wider cultural values; in this book the censorship of art does not require consideration in its own right.

The general point which I wish to emerge from the argument above is a simple one: we cannot take what is superficially the area of restrictive activity as helping us very much to make a classification of censorship, for the ostensible area which it purports to concern may not be the same as the area which it materially affects. If censorship is to be classified into different types we shall have to adopt a less naive approach, using the apparent area of censorship as, perhaps, contributory evidence, but giving our final attention to its motivations, its aims or its purposes, and its actual consequences. It is to the possibility of a demarcation of classes of censorship along these lines that I now wish to turn.

Justifications

National Security

I am citing this reason for censorship first because it stands apart from other reasons. It does so insofar as in appropriate circumstances it seems that its principle—though not the extent of that principle—is beyond dispute, except for those who would have no truck with the state whatsoever. In this context it is not necessary to discuss the nature of all possible 'appropriate' circumstances; it is enough that on any interpretation the possibility of such circumstances is conceivable. Nevertheless, the conception of national security which I am suggesting here need only be a minimal one, limited in the following way. First, it presupposes a state or political structure of some kind, which its citizens or members desire to maintain; second, security is required against an external enemy—the problem of an internal threat is a different one and properly considered under the headings of public order and the preservation of society; third, the censorship enforced is the minimum amount believed in good faith to be required to prevent direct or indirect assistance to the external enemy—that is to say, national security is not properly used either as a pretext for the extension of interference and restrictions into many apparently unconnected areas of life or as an excuse for withholding from the citizens of the state information about matters of largely internal significance.

This conception of censorship in the interests of national security seems, in the minimum it provides, beyond dispute if initial support is granted for the idea that an independent self-governing society and its associated state merit some assurance of their continuing existence. The acknowledgment in principle of the permissibility of censorship in this area says nothing, of course, about any further rules which should govern its administration or any safeguards against its abuse.

Disputes about censorship for reasons of national security seem to be based on practice rather than principle, on claims that it is abused or, even more commonly, that its actual extent is too considerable for its own declared terms of reference. In contrast, all other forms of censorship are contentious in principle. Their justifications and purposes, together with those of other restrictions of freedom, relate, I believe, to several apparently distinct categories, which will be considered individually: truth, right opinion, good taste and the giving of offence, majority opinion, public order, and the preservation of society.

Truth

The protection of truth and the suppression of error have from time to time been major grounds for policies of censorship. Ironically, the discovery of truth and the eradication of error have also provided grounds for arguments against censorship. I will discuss the strengths and weaknesses of these kinds of arguments later in the book and therefore offer no comment for the time being on the rights and wrongs of a policy which uses censorship to protect what is believed to be the truth against supposed error. The argument for the protection of truth has been used to justify restrictions in empirical areas of human knowledge, but has had a more notable function in the past in matters of religion, where it now seems a more questionable justification of restrictive measures. Where sceptical, relativist or pluralist tendencies are strong in a society, it is clear that arguments for restrictions in the name of truth are going to be unconvincing.

Right Opinion

The mention of religion raises the question how far the protection of belief can be argued for in the same terms as the protection of knowledge. With reference to religious claims there has often in the past been no principle of distinction made between knowledge and belief: religious truth has had the same status as what we now regard as kinds of scientific, if not mathematical, truth and knowledge. At times, indeed, the latter have been subordinated to it. But the tenets of religion, in particular (for Western societies) Christianity, have brought with them certain claims about proper morality and other forms of social organization and behaviour. While the substance of these claims is regarded by many as incapable of being factually true or false, it may be that they are considered both to be demanded by the system of religious beliefs dominant in a society and to be necessary for the maintenance of that system and the society which is structurally characterized by it. The preservation of right opinion in matters of morality thus becomes necessary for the very survival of society.[11]

Mutatis mutandis, other kinds of belief—historical or mythological, for example—could assume the role of religious beliefs after this fashion. If certain beliefs seem essential to the structure of society, censorship may be considered a justifiable practice in the interests of the maintenance of right opinion and the preservation of a society when its essential character appears to be threatened. The maintenance of right opinion is thus justified in two ways: by its conceptual connection with what are believed to be truths, and by its teleological connection with the preservation of society. This possible justification will be considered last of all.

Good Taste and the Giving of Offence

I suggested that right opinion could be linked to the idea of truth, especially given such an idea—one less widespread than formerly—as that of religious or moral truth. It is equally possible that there is a general notion of right opinion which is not linked to any concept of truth, but which is made evident through prevailing social attitudes. Such attitudes also give rise to conceptions of good taste and often seem to determine what kinds of things are found offensive. Insofar as good taste is tied to attitudes that have no connection, even indirect, with truth however conceived, justification of censorship linked to truth cannot be used. Censorship applied according to the criteria of good taste in order to prevent the giving of offence can then be justified, in the main, only by saying that expressions of certain opinions, or presentations of certain subject-matters, would give offence to a majority of people or to a minority of some significance (not necessarily in numbers) or are held offensive by a body of experts or an authoritative elite (especially judges, members of parliament, or government ministers) of some kind.

When good taste is linked to majority opinion the corresponding ground for limiting freedom of expression is simply the majoritarian principle. When good taste depends on the judgment of a body of experts or an elite there is recognition that certain persons deserve respect for their pronouncements on taste because they are thought to be superior in such matters, through, for example, having a greater degree of knowledge, experience or ability. In such cases there is belief in a form of well-grounded opinion and judgment, a quasi-objective concept of good taste independent of the feelings of a large number of people. As a justification of censorship such a concept of good taste may be related to beliefs about truth and right opinion. In the matter of offensiveness it is possible that censorship will be imposed to avoid the giving of offence not simply to the majority but to virtually any fair number of people at all (although it would be impossible, obviously, to avoid offence being taken on some occasions by a small number of people). Such action (as, for example, with race relations) will be determined by a particular conception of society as well as by a desire to preserve public order.

Majority Opinion

The 'tyranny of the majority' is a well-worn phrase. If applied to the majority's support for a policy of censorship merely to carry out its own wishes in its own interests, it would seem a fair enough description. However, if majoritarian principles were followed consistently in the state, they would be as adequate a justification of censorship as of any other policy. Their imposition could only be countered by an appeal that freedom of speech occupies some privileged position to which majoritarian principles are inapplicable; this appeal would suitably be located within a more comprehensive theory of the limits of governmental power generally—as indeed it is in liberal democracies.

Majority opinion is most evident in the matter of what is considered to be in good taste—or at least not in bad taste—and also in the suppression of eccentric, unpopular or 'dangerous' ideas.

Public Order

Public order is arguably the most generally acceptable justification for censorship after national security. As an excuse for minimal censorship it seems unexceptionable when the term 'public order' is sparingly interpreted. A restriction on freedom of speech, when that freedom is to be used to make direct incitement to riot, can hardly be objected to under normal conditions. However, the concept is capable of considerable extension, and suitable circumstances for the exercise of restrictions are subject to varying interpretations. The rationale of the maintenance of public order is found in its thoroughly physical representation of the breakdown of norms of social organization; disorder foreshadows the total breakdown of society in a concrete way. The concept of public order and its extensions will receive fuller discussion at a later point.[12] The intimate connections between public order, social organization and the nature of society brings us directly to the last possible justification of censorship to be considered, namely the preservation of society.

Preserving Society

Measures of censorship are frequently intended to contribute to the long-term preservation of the form of society and the conservation of what seems essential to its structure, such that if that structure were destroyed or perverted, the society would itself be changed so radically that it would have lost continuity with its predecessor. The victim of censorship is seen by the authorities to represent, through the opinions he expresses or the information he communicates, a threat to the established social structure and organization. Censorship is predominantly conservative; it acts against those who directly or implicitly challenge the society's assumptions. In this sense it always seeks to preserve even when it is exercised by revolutionary regimes against conservative opinions, for the latter represent a threat to the continuity and survival of the revolutionary social structure. The previous categories of possible justifications and purposes of censorship, although they have much interest in their own right, relate also to what belongs to an established social order. The point of reference of censorship is 'the governing authority' or 'the social or moral order'.[13] It is an exaggeration, perhaps, but not a distortion to assert that in the end, with only a few exceptions, 'all censorship is political censorship'.[14] An attack on truth, or on what is believed to be truth, might be seen as putting at risk a value that is absolute, but it is more realistically understood as representing a threat to the society for which adherence to truth—and a particular conception of 'truth' at that—is essential. Even good taste is related to deeply held social attitudes, although its superficial manifestations may appear both conventional and trivial.

Censorship is an important way in which a society seeks to preserve its social order and integrity against the threats embodied in dissent, many eccentric or innovative ideas, and the unwelcome dissemination of some kinds of information. In particular it is believed to protect a society against the social fragmentation that may be brought about by a generally free access to competitive ideas.

What is meant by 'social order' and 'integrity' in this connection? A few words are necessary to elucidate terms which might otherwise seem nebulous and questionable abstractions, or might be misunderstood. The concept of social order does not refer to the social order as that term is commonly understood in the sense of the established class structure, although in most cases, clearly, such a class structure will constitute part of the essential structure of society and contribute to social order. Nor is 'social order' to be confused with 'public order'; it does not refer specifically to 'law and order' in their relation to physical security, although, again, the maintenance of public order will make an important contribution to it. Social order is what characterizes an ordered and orderly society; it refers in the widest sense to the structure and organization of society, to the form under which it functions. A threat to social order is a threat to the current organization of society and its continued cohesion with a similar character. Certain measures—and censorship is one of them—seek to perpetuate the essence of society as this is somehow enshrined in its basic structure, its general scheme of values (those values adhered to in principle if not obviously in practice by most members of a society), and the aims and beliefs of its members. In this regard conservatism does not entail stasis; the structure of society can be such as not simply to permit but to require development and progress along certain lines. Restrictions on free speech suggest a static society, certainly; but it is possible at least to conceive a censorship directed towards progress, run along lines to eliminate potentially retrogressive opinions and ideas and suppress attitudes perceived as detrimental to progress, even though it might be argued that it would in practice defeat its own ends.

By my use of the word 'integrity' I mean that the conception of society—the conception of *their* society—will be defined for its members by reference to certain parameters; it will be characterized by basic and conceptually inalienable features and principles. In Western societies at the present time, 'integrity' makes reference to certain fundamental ideas of political ethics, notably those of liberal democracy.[15] The current conception that people have of their society will be manifested in what they do and say, in the way they typically behave, in their common attitudes and general expectations. Any conception can incorporate change of a kind and up to a point, but some kinds of change, and change beyond a certain point, will result either in its breakdown or its metamorphosis into an essentially different concept.

Plainly, certain ideas have from time to time changed a society so deeply as to lead to the revolutionary development of, essentially, a new society. Continuity there may be, but it seems of little consequence, and for a long time it is often obscured by numerous innovative social features. If it is evident that the successful dissemination and adoption of new ideas throughout a society would effectively destroy it, the suppression of a potential source of destruction will ensure that new ideas cannot be adopted and thus safeguard society's continued existence in its present form. The preservation of society is a rational course of action for a governing authority to adopt and for those who make up a society to support.

Unity of Purpose

On a surface analysis it seems that censorship has many different aims and objects, with distinguishable rationales in diverse areas of operation. I have cited the most important of these above and suggested that superficial distinctions of censorship may have no significance for an understanding of the true purposes of restrictions. However, it is still possible that at a deeper level separate policies of censorship may be unrelated. How distinct may separate restrictive actions against free speech really be in the end?

It is an individualistic point of view which favours the belief that censorship is of a multifarious nature. When individuals and their rights are paramount in social and political thinking different kinds of censorship seem to be unconnected, even *ad hoc*, measures in relation to any putative common principle. From a more holistic and collective viewpoint—one which gives intrinsic importance to the collective life of society and the groups and interrelationships that make it up—different forms of censorship become bound up with ideas about social expression and how that expression is to be defined and regulated, so that where policies of censorship are not vestigial survivals of earlier measures but are reasonably comprehsive and intended to be effective, a single rationale can plausibly be advanced and developed.

The person for whom religion, morality and politics occupy (so to speak) separate compartments will believe religious censorship, political censorship and moral censorship to be separate policies, affecting him or her in distinct areas of life, and having few internal links. Individually, that person relates such policies, for the most part, to his or her own life, and does not see how they are (or should be) integrated into the life of society as a whole. In a social context the interrelationship of different policies becomes more evident. An ostensibly religious custom may continue to survive in a central position, after the religion that gave rise to it has lost universal acceptance, because it retains or acquires a social significance. What Lord Devlin had to say about marriage is illustrative of the relationship of many moral, religious and other customs to the nature of the society in which they are found, when for the individual the connection has been entirely lost. He wrote that the Christian institution of marriage 'has become the basis of family life and so part of the structure of our society'.

Although it still apparently makes appeal to specific religious beliefs, it is not there now because it is Christian: 'It has got there because it is Christian, but it remains there because it is built into the house in which we live and could not be removed without bringing it down.'[16]

Too great an emphasis on individualism obscures the social importance of many kinds of rules and customs, especially moral and political ones. Censorship in many areas seeks to actualize some of these rules, and to regulate social behaviour in many areas according to them. This is not to say that all censorship falls readily into a pattern of what may be called social reinforcement. Some of it may in its principles be no more than its appearance suggests, that is, at the worst, no more than an *ad hoc* or arbitrary measure. However, I am making the claim that censorship is not to be classified *primarily* along lines of subject or area, by the methods used, in terms of a distinction between expression, information or communication, or according to whether it is a pre- or post-publication measure.

The primary classification, therefore, is between those policies of censorship which are measures initiated to serve some immediate practical need, and those which can be linked to social purposes (of whatever kind) and are therefore capable of justification in terms of them. (Note that this does not mean that the instigators or executors of censorship with a social purpose must have given a great deal of conscious thought to the possible aims of their policies.) Which type of censorship has importance for a society and how different methods may be effective in different societies are not questions to be answered theoretically in advance. What matters to a society will vary: for one it will be political expression; for a second, religious adherence; for a third, moral attitudes. Whether pre-publication censorship is tolerable will again be determined by social attitudes and by the way in which such a policy fits in with and caters for the society in question.

In support of policies serving an immediate practical purpose the arguments of the opponents of censorship can hardly be met, let alone refuted. With no social justification, individualistic claims must be conceded. But given the social justification for many apparently diverse forms of censorship, the area of conflict between individual and society is entered at a high level. A large part of the argument about censorship must be decided according to the several degrees of importance allotted to social needs and aims and the manner in which the fundamental nature of a cohering community is conceived.

Notes

1 H.D. Lasswell, 'Censorship', in *Encyclopedia of the Social Sciences* (New York, 1930–35), Vol. III, p. 290.

2 At the time of writing, the proposed Freedom of Information Bill for the United Kingdom is an excellent exemplar of these tendencies.

3 The boundaries of the public domain may shift considerably, but they are bound to remain a contested area so long as there is an excluded area at all.

4 Nevertheless, as far as the United Kingdom is concerned, the possession of a certificate (or lack of it) is not finally determinative of the issue of obscenity in law.

5 The problem of social control of this kind is peculiarly taxing. It was one of the *bêtes noires* of Herbert Marcuse (among others); see especially his essay, 'Repressive tolerance', in Robert Paul Wolff *et al.*, *A Critique of Pure Tolerance* (London, 1969), pp. 95–137.

6 See Frederick Schauer, *Free speech: a philosophical enquiry* (Cambridge, 1982), p. 16.

7 For an extended treatment of the Rushdie affair in a manner appropriate to the theme of this book see Simon Lee, *The Cost of Free Speech* (London, 1990), Part IV: 'Salman Rushdie and The Satanic Verses'.

8 Richard Dawkins is one of the most outspoken advocates of this position.

9 Where nevertheless the half-forgotten offence of seditious libel—'to excite British subjects to attempt otherwise than by lawful means the alteration of any matter in Church or State by law'—is still on the statute book. (See further Paul O'Higgins, *Censorship in Britain* (London, 1972), p. 34.)

10 See Patrick Devlin, *The Enforcement of Morals* (London, 1965), p. 13.

11 *Cf.* Devlin, *op. cit.*, pp. 13–14. The argument finds echoes at the present time in political debate.

12 The preservation of public order extends by degrees into the prevention of subversion. I take this extension up later in chapter 4.

13 *Cf.* Lasswell's definition of censorship cited above.

14 William Seagle, quoted in O'Higgins, *op. cit.*, p. 15.

15 I take the concept of integrity from Dworkin: see *Law's Empire* (London, 1986), chapter 6.

16 Devlin, *op. cit.*, p. 9.

2 Criticisms of Censorship

The Needs of Truth

Censorship tends to arouse in many people, without further consideration of its context or purpose, an immediate feeling of disapproval. This is especially the case when what is assumed to be censorship affects the expression of serious intellectual pursuits or sincerely held political opinions. Nevertheless, many people also dislike apparent or actual censorship in more trivial matters, although with respect to these there is a greater diversity of opinion as to what sorts of materials may or should be modified, restricted or banned.

Opposition to the limiting of self-expression has a long history, and past arguments against censorship often retain a *prima facie* validity today. On analysis some soon appear to be mistaken; others, however, require more thoughtful treatment. All are both interesting in themselves and important in bringing up for discussion some other values which have a bearing on policies affecting free speech.

Free Speech and Truth

The protection of truth has been used as a justification of censorship and other restrictive policies; the most prominent example historically is of course, the Catholic Church's maintenance of the *Index Librorum Prohibitorum* from the Middle Ages down to the present century in its endeavours to protect religious truth from corruption as well as to safeguard the moral welfare of the faithful—a course of action which can offer publicity to intellectually stimulating works just as to those providing stimulation of a more salacious kind. It has also been commonly claimed that censorship is disadvantageous to the cause of truth and that it is the free situation which really protects the value of truth. Two arguments on these lines have sometimes been accepted as presenting decisive objections to censorship.

The first argument claims that in a free situation truth will, in the long run at least, prevail over falsehood, that the better argument will be preferred to the worse. Truth will prevail: 'Let her and Falshood grapple; who ever knew Truth put to the wors, in a free and open encounter?'[1] In support of Milton's words we may add the equally sure claim of Oliver Wendell Holmes that 'the best test of truth is the power of the thought to get itself accepted in the competition of the market'.[2] As a text for our 'postmodern' era this easily becomes the belief that truth is what gets accepted in the market-place.[3] Frederick Schauer has pointed out that freedom of speech can be likened to the process of cross-examination, and therefore this aspect of the argument from the value of truth can be said to rest partly on the success of an adversarial process as a means of discovering truth.[4] Unfortunately, recent experience is not such as to encourage optimism about this. The exposure of miscarriages of justice—which is itself no argument in favour of censorship—suggests that to compare the struggle between truth and falsehood (in an atmosphere of free speech) with a contest in a court of law depends on a dubious and unhappy analogy.

In short, for some people at least, censorship in the interest of the protection of truth, however well-intentioned it may be, has seemed to be unnecessary. This claim needs no more than a passing mention for it to be exposed as a clear case of wishful thinking; the power of deception has been recognized since Plato inveighed against the Sophists. Truth, especially in the abstract world of ideas, could not compel us to accept it of its own accord on every occasion; it could not do so even in a world of perfectly rational people who strove always to act in good faith, for even then some people would encounter difficulties in accepting some 'new' truth because of their incomplete knowledge of relevant supporting information.

Success for truth depends on the rhetorical power of its advocate. The person who advances false beliefs and mistaken ideas may be the superior manipulator. In a free market evil will from time to time prevail over good; this statement needs no support other than the suggestion that doubters should consult their history books. But there is a less easily dismissed corollary to the argument just mentioned. This is that if errors, superstitions, false opinions, and similar wrong ideas are only left alone in a situation in which they are free and open to the truth, even if they prevail for a while, they will eventually die a natural death. The distinction between the two arguments lies in the difference that there is between an active and a passive error. Benjamin Constant, for example, wrote that 'superstition is deeply harmful only when it is protected or threatened', and if it is unprovoked, 'it will become an innocent passion and will then soon die'.[5]

Obviously this is an argument which stands or falls on observation, and so not one with which a theoretical study need be overly concerned. As an empirical argument it would seem that ample evidence might be found to refute it. In everyday affairs, ethically trivial though they often are, in the absence of any pressures one way or the other, one can see all too often the inferior preferred to the qualitatively superior, the inconsequential to the serious and considered, the bland to the disturbing or properly stimulating. Superstition and irrationality continue to thrive. In more serious matters many people clearly prefer to remain with their confirmed beliefs, holding on to whatever has always seemed right to them, and keeping their minds closed to reasoned argument. Taking a longer historical perspective does not encourage optimism.

In actuality truth is not always bound to triumph over falsehood, nor good over evil. False beliefs seem unlikely to languish away for lack of attention, for in a free society they receive all too much. To suggest that truth is certain, or even just very likely, to prevail over falsehood, to claim that errors and superstitions will, if left alone, cease to exercise power over beliefs and actions, and simply die away, is to suppose a state of affairs that does not exist, given people as they are. Such claims are dangerous, both for the intellectual value of truth, and the good order of society. Those who argue in support of a wide and unrestricted freedom of expression must abandon their optimism and recognize that the policies they advocate will not lead automatically to the adoption of new truths and better values, while leaving existing accepted truths and good values unharmed. Such policies may enable us only to discover in vain those worthwhile ideas and opinions which would otherwise remain unknown to us. There remains therefore a plausible case for well-intentioned censorship kept in place as the guardian of what is believed in good faith to be the truth. However, other arguments against censorship may yet rebut the arguments in favour of this role.

The Danger of Suppressing Truth

The discussion of the preceding section centred on considerations of an empirical kind. It is a matter of fact that truth does not always prevail in this world, and it is conceivable that it would not always do so even in the best of free societies while human nature retains its present character. If we consider a related argument we encounter problems of a more philosophical kind. This second argument is that we should not be prepared through the enforcement of restrictive policies to risk the possible, though unwitting, suppression of the truth. One fundamental reason for the advocacy of the widest liberty is that the opinion we suppress may possibly be true; no censoring authority, even though it acts in utmost good faith, can lay claim to infallibility in its actions.[6]

Is this a decisive argument against censorship or a deterrent to the limitation of free speech? That great advocate of free speech John Stuart Mill conveniently set down the counter-argument to his own position, pointing out that for governments to prohibit harmful expression

> is not claiming exemption from error, but fulfilling the duty incumbent on them, although fallible, of acting on their conscientious conviction. ... Men, and governments, must act to the best of their ability. There is no such thing as absolute certainty, but there is assurance sufficient for the purpose of human life. We may, and must, assume our opinion to be true for the guidance of our own conduct: and it is assuming no more when we forbid bad men to pervert society by the propagation of opinions which we regard as false or pernicious.[7]

Mill did not give sufficient attention to some of the implications of the argument that he presents here, particularly as it is stated on a largely individualistic level, that is to say, in terms of *our* opinions in opposition to the opinions of others. Even in individualistic terms the argument has more to be said for it, and it is a stronger argument still when it is restated in the context of social organization. I shall have more to say on the social aspects involved at a later stage.

A Distinction of Principles

It is in order at this point to indicate and comment on a significant distinction made in Mill's retort to his own devil's advocate. He refers to the difference that there is 'between presuming an opinion to be true, because, with every opportunity for contesting it, it has not been refuted, and assuming its truth for the purpose of not permitting its refutation'.[8] In other words, there is a difference between an opinion, belief or principle which has been, and is still, open to free discussion and possible modification or refutation, and one about which no worthwhile or significant debate is allowed.

It would be incorrect to think that Mill himself would have agreed with the consequences which I believe to be suggested by his ideas. Yet it may be contended that by following up the implications of Mill's distinction we are provided with a useful means of assessing the permissibility of different types and instances of censorship. Mill's distinction implicitly permits censorship and restriction of liberty to a substantial degree. Its consequence is that an appropriate authority is entitled in good faith to engage in a particular act of suppression as long as the principle governing its action remains open to debate. In other words, the only form of curtailment of expression that cannot be allowed at all is the suppression of arguments against a specific policy of censorship or about the principle underlying such a policy.

However, there is a yet stronger position to be adopted from Mill's distinction. It would not be enough that arguments against censorship were considerable in their weight and support; acceptance of them would only be mandatory when the supposedly justifying principles of a particular form of censorship were shown to fail. A principle of action may be presumed true when, in Mill's words, 'with every opportunity for contesting it, it has not been refuted'.[9] Censorship can continue while it remains a subject for debate. 'Complete liberty of contradicting and disproving our opinion,' Mill wrote, 'is the very condition which justifies us in assuming its truth for purposes of action'.[10] This statement can now be interpreted in such a way as to possess a more positive force than Mill ever intended. If the restriction of certain liberties—notably, here, censorship—in a particular area and following a certain principle, is believed right and proper, then an authority is justified in assuming the truth of the principle underlying the restriction and in acting on that assumption, provided that other people are at liberty at least to discuss and question that principle.[11]

Making use of Mill's distinction we may distinguish two categories of expression open to censorship. On the one hand there are opinions and beliefs about certain rights and freedoms. On the other there are actions, expressions of opinions, and ways of speaking and writing, which in their content display the results of holding those opinions or beliefs. The distinction may be more easily understood if I illustrate it with some examples. The free distribution of pornography could be the consequence of an opinion (not necessarily held very consciously or explicitly) about the principle of sexual freedom or of a belief about the true nature of obscenity;

blasphemous expression (by which is meant in this context the expression of more or less rational and considered ideas formerly accounted blasphemous) results from, or manifests, an opinion about the principle of religious and atheistic freedom; again, the absence of film censorship in a state would be an instantiation of a belief in complete freedom of expression.

On the one hand, then, there are opinions, beliefs and principles; on the other there are their practical consequences. Following the refutability principle, as it may be called, which can be developed from one understanding of what Mill suggests, it is permissible to ban the practical expressions or consequences of a belief or opinion so long as the theoretical principle which forms the basis of that belief (or the opinion itself) remains open to discussion. And this is a condition that holds in many areas in our own society: motion pictures in the United Kingdom, for example, are subjected to scrutiny and cut, but the principle of film censorship can be openly debated; libel is illegal, but we can, if we choose, still attempt to argue a case against its unlawfulness or for its redefinition. A concrete example of what cannot be permitted under the refutability principle is provided by a typical state of affairs in some countries where literary freedom is severely curtailed: in addition to numerous instances of censorship and other restrictions affecting action and expression there are to be found extensive prohibitions on discussions about literary freedom and even on suggestions that an overstrict and unwelcome censorship may exist.[12]

The principle advanced here is that in discussions about censorship of obscenity, for example, there is a distinction to be drawn between what are basically opinions about what counts as obscenity and whether obscenity is rightly prohibited and actual obscene expressions; or, in discussions of political censorship, between opinions about whether the publication of subversive ideas should be allowed and public expression of those ideas. This may seem an obvious and simple distinction but, I suggest, it is not one which is always clearly discernible when the subject of debate is a problem like the proper extent of freedom of speech or the acceptability of censorship.

There is, certainly, one awkward objection that can be made against the workability of this distinction; this is that the ability to discuss fruitfully and positively a principle of censorship requires full knowledge of particular instances that it covers, and that thereby any 'reasonable' censorship invalidates itself. A genuine argument about censorship, that is to say, requires a direct acquaintance with prospective candidates for censorship. However, it is not evident that this is the case. What is required for an argument about censorship to be properly conducted is not knowledge of actual censorable material but of what such censorable material may be like, not a direct acquaintance with actual totally free situations but of what a situation where there were no restrictions might resemble. The information required need not depend on the use of imagination to any great extent, nor need decisions be taken on the basis of *a priori* reasoning or essentially speculative ideas grounded in insufficient information of an empirical kind. One can compare the present situation with the past, where conditions were different regarding the amount and type of censorship; or one can contrast the present society with others which have more or less censorship and other restrictions than one's own. And if censorship is being imposed afresh rather than merely being continued, it is clear that there would be common acquaintance with the object of restrictions, and therefore adequate material for debate about the principle.

It is by allowing the *principle* of suppression to be freely discussed, that truth is safeguarded, if only indirectly. I emphasize that this is certainly not the sort of conclusion that Mill would wish us to infer from his argument. Nevertheless, on one interpretation it is a reasonable extension of his argument. Furthermore, it seems to provide an adequate arrangement for the operation of censorship. Society and government can allow debates about the merits and demerits of a specific restrictive law, just as they can about any other law, all the while enforcing that law strictly. In this way censorship in a given area and a basic freedom of opinion about that area can coexist, although it is undeniable that complete freedom of expression is not present. In such a situation there would always be a possibility, and a fairly realistic one, that laws imposing restrictions could undergo amendment or repeal.

Because the law imposing censorship may itself always be brought into question in this situation, the permanent loss of truth or valuable ideas and opinions need not be feared: what are believed to be the social, moral or other benefits of a proper policy of censorship intended to be sincerely constructive may still be retained. A great danger to society and the individual comes when the *principle* of censorship in a particular area cannot be the subject of free discussion. Then the permanent loss to society of valuable opinion and knowledge may rightly be feared. Yet it should not be forgotten that although with any measure of censorship we always *risk* suppressing the truth, we ought also to succeed in suppressing much that would undoubtedly be pernicious to society and its members. For the consequentialist—who must be prepared to take one thing with another—censorship may provide a net benefit for society. The usefulness of censorship in preserving and strengthening a certain kind of society and in contributing to public order remains to be discussed.[13]

The foregoing argument has been intended to show how restrictions on freedom of expression in the interests of public order or public decency, that is, in support of values other than truth, limit rather than destroy that freedom. And although they limit it, they do not inflict permanent loss if the rationale of the restrictions remains open to debate, as it may do while the restrictions themselves remain in force. It shows also how an active concern for order or decency as well as for truth may be at least partially reconciled with a belief in freedom.

Two Further Questions

The importance of truth and its use in arguments against censorship and in support of the most unrestricted free speech raise two sets of questions which are largely ignored by those arguments. The first set of questions worries about consequences. What are we to say about the acceptability of censorship if it is agreed that, no matter how well-regulated the situation, it is possible for truth to yield to falsehood and for evil to prevail over good? This seems not only a conceivable occurrence, but it is also one that has occurred often enough in the past. Is it better that truth should cede to falsehood in a maximally free society than that it should survive in a less free one? The answer to this question must rest on a consideration of the general advantages of extensive freedom to society and their possible outweighing of setbacks for truth, public order, or social cohesion in individual cases.[14]

The second set of questions concerns the apparent indiscriminate attitude to values in a society with maximal freedom. How is truth in general strengthened? Is it strengthened by the avoidance of all restrictive policies (beyond the bare minimum required to suppress threats of immediate and serious disorder)? Or is truth strengthened as a whole by the realization that certain values are to be preferred to others, that these values create the conditions for a progressive enrichment of our knowledge and beliefs and our general way of life? If it is recognized that the features of society in which these preferred values are realized may not survive in an atmosphere of free competition, then they surely require to be given selective advantages (which may involve the use of discriminatory measures, either directly or indirectly, against such features as embody other values). If certain values are qualitatively superior, or even if they are only believed to be so, it seems impossible that those who subscribe to that belief could allow them to succumb in the end to those values believed to be inferior. Once it is granted that the outcome in the struggle between truth and falsehood may not be a victory for truth, the disadvantages of a total free speech may assume significant proportions. It is salutary to remember that truth and superior values have not always prevailed.

The Arbitrary and Capricious Nature of Censorship

For many people restrictions of censorship largely represent arbitrary and often capricious interference with personal freedoms.[15] The implication seems to be that unless there is a total ban on all examples of a type of subject-matter or expression of opinion there should be no censorship at all; otherwise censorship will only encourage an observance of the letter of the law rather than its spirit. It is possible for writers and artists to work their way around a censorship law by attempting to preserve the substance of what they want to say while avoiding surface forms of expression which would expose them to legal penalties; for their part censors, perhaps through insensitivity, obtuseness, or bureaucratic muddle, are likely to apply the law in a literalistic fashion, forbidding or mutilating samples of effectively harmless material, yet at the same time allowing a significant proportion of dangerous or objectionable items (in their terms) which happens to be expressed in a subtle, sophisticated or devious manner to be published without hindrance.

All this may be true; but the point not to be missed is that, as it stands, this is not an argument against censorship in principle. It would only be an argument against the very idea of censorship if it were also claimed that censorship *necessarily* involved arbitrary or capricious interference with personal freedoms. In the initial form stated above, the development of the argument presents us only with an objection to arbitrary or capricious censorship which is quite on a par with objections to arbitrary or capricious taxation, personal searches, or arrests for motoring offences. There can be no question that laws which are arbitrary or capricious in formulation or execution are generally to be deprecated. But for censorship generally to be disapproved, it must be shown that it has to be intrinsically arbitrary or capricious.[16] It will be useful if I first look at ways in which a policy of censorship may happen to be so in its working; after that I shall go on to examine whether any of these arbitrary or capricious workings of censorship are necessarily entailed either by our concept of censorship or by the ways in which censorship has to be practised.

Arbitrary Censorship

Censorship, like taxation, can often be avoided (legally) or evaded (illegally). Faced with the obstacle of censorship, the skilful writer, editor or publisher can achieve limited success from time to time in attempts to have the substance of a book or article published without too much change, while the less fortunate individual, who adopts a more ingenuous approach, will find his work savagely cut or altogether prohibited. Some writers may present their ideas as fable or fantasy and have them pass the censor unscathed, while others, expressing themselves in literal language or representing their ideas in a realistic way, will have their work emasculated or banned. In the last few years more liberal attitudes towards sexual material have prevailed, but until recently, so long as pornography could be presented as a work of science, medicine or social research—or even as 'erotica'—it had a chance of being published and distributed in a limited way, when similar material presented as no more than what it really was would usually be seized and destroyed with no more than a perfunctory court hearing if police action was even challenged. Under a restrictive regime, the revolutionary philosopher may advance his ideas in the form of a historical critique, which passes the censor unnoticed, while the same ideas openly discussed in a contemporary context are immediately suppressed.

Patently such practices must be judged arbitrary, because the censorship in practice does not realize consistently the intent of the principle supposed to underlie it. As far as both their efficacy and fairness are concerned, we could say that the censors might as well select likely works for prohibition at random. Ultimately they fail to justify their actions by acting in ways that are wholly consistent with their stated principles.

An arbitrary application of a policy may well be a common fault whenever censorship is practised. It may come about not only through the intentional manoeuvres of serious writers, artists and thinkers, as well as the purveyors of more prurient material, but also without any purposeful actions on the censors' part when they fail to carry out their work thoroughly. (As I shall show shortly, the latter type of case may also be open to the charge of capriciousness.) The philosopher's unacceptable opinions may just happen to be expressed in the shape of a historical study because that is what he was engaged on at the time, and not because he was seeking to get his arguments past the censors in disguise. The writer may himself be a staunch believer in the principles governing a policy of censorship and a direct supporter of restrictions; he might be as alarmed as the authorities if deviant work of his were not modified, rewritten or even, where necessary, abandoned.

The failure to perceive that certain material warrants censorship is of course most likely to happen when the censors have insufficient knowledge, experience and training to know in sufficient depth what they are dealing with; and this must often be the case.[17] The problems presented by a contingent lack of aptitude, however, have no bearing on the principle of censorship; they are practical problems, and insofar as they are no more than that, they can be remedied (in theory) by training the censors in the skills which are necessary for them to carry out their work in the most effective fashion.

Capricious Censorship

In terms of their conceptual logic arbitrary actions and capricious actions are not entirely distinct. Therefore, for the purposes of this discussion, by an 'arbitrary' action I mean one that is done without reason, or one done without being consistently related to the matter in hand so that it appears to be done without reason. This concept of arbitrariness should have been adequately brought out in the remarks of the foregoing section. By a 'capricious' action is meant one that is governed by whim; a capricious censorship will be one that is dependent on the vagaries of the censors. The censor may be faced with more material than he can handle in a thorough fashion; therefore he may carry out savage cuts on a relatively small number of items as an example to others. So long as sanctions are severe enough, so long as the proportion of material looked at is high enough and operations maintained at a visible level, the deterrent effect and the encouragement of self-censorship are likely to be worthwhile from the censor's point of view. The result of such a selective process is not likely to be a total compliance with censorship laws, but there should be created a situation where problematic material for the censor will be no more than he can conveniently deal with.

Such measures are certainly capricious, but their capriciousness, so long as the initial selection of material is a random one, is not of itself unfair; in being random it is not deliberately biased, and methods will usually be dictated by practical exigencies. Any random checks involved would be similar to those carried out by customs and tax authorities, which equally are not considered unfair in principle, but are seen as a selective approach to a problem dictated by practicalities.

However, capriciousness can be manifested in an unfair way. There is the capriciousness of victimization, a policy of deliberately picking on certain individuals and their works, on certain groups and organizations and their activities. There is also the capriciousness shown in periodic fluctuations in the level and extent of censorship, with the result that particular individuals and groups may never be sure where they stand. Such states of affairs may typically arise when repressive measures are activated by external threats or by the uncertain sensitivities of those in power. Unfairly based measures require no further treatment, since it is to be accepted as axiomatic that at all times the law is to be applied fairly and indifferently to everybody, and as reasonably as possible, however seldom this may be the case in practice.

Is Censorship Necessarily Arbitrary or Capricious?

Having clarified the characteristics of arbitrary and capricious censorship, I now address the question whether censorship of necessity embodies such limitations and failings. Capriciousness is conceptually a term to be ascribed to the behaviour of individual people. To act capriciously is to be guided by a whim, and, by the logic of the word, a whim cannot be written into law or set down in any formal fashion: that would be to ground it in a rule and thereby contradict the very idea of caprice. Capriciousness is not a word that can describe a necessary feature of an abstract concept or a principle of behaviour. Therefore censorship can never be capricious in principle but can only be so in practice, and then because of the capricious actions of its executors. It is the interpreters and executors of censorship, those who give effect to a law or policy, who may act capriciously. No law, principle or policy of censorship, of any substance, can itself be capricious. An accusation of capriciousness, though apparently levelled at a policy of censorship, can be correctly made in criticism only of censors and their practice, and not of either a principle of censorship or censorship in principle.

May censorship be inherently or essentially arbitrary? The word 'arbitrary' here is intended to convey not the idea that actions have no guiding principle but, rather more, that the apparent absence of principle is due to the use of guidelines substantially unconnected with proffered justifications. It may be that censorship necessarily is applied in such a way that what is done for ostensibly intrinsic reasons can only be carried out according to extrinsic criteria. An example, which has figured from time to time in the obscenity laws of various jurisdictions, is the pedantic listing of parts of the body which may not be exposed in visual material. Obviously this measure can fail to stop a significant amount of obscene material being published whenever it can pass the literal-minded test which is set; it also fails to prevent the portrayal of an adequately clothed body in a pornographic or obscene fashion.

To put the problem another way: although plainly there is a 'spirit' to any law or principle of censorship, may it nevertheless *necessarily* be the case that censorship can only be carried out efficiently according to the 'letter' of the law? Censorship is necessarily arbitrary, it seems, only in two kinds of situation: borderline cases constitute one kind, and states of conceptual uncertainty the other—these latter are exemplified when the attitudes motivating restrictions are in general decline or undergoing radical change in a particular society.

Borderline Cases

Necessarily arbitrary applications of censorship occur in borderline cases. I offer little comment on the concept of borderline cases here. Their characterization as problem cases for the application of concepts is a familiar one, and familiar too is the confusion into which borderline cases can lead us if we are not careful always to remember that they are just *borderline* cases and do not automatically provide examples to threaten the central core of a given concept.[18] With appropriate knowledge and experience, with even average education and intelligence, in a society where the core of the relevant concept is not in dispute, we should easily be able to recognize truly subversive material, an obscene drawing, a libellous description or, for that matter, a book which possesses redeeming social value. Yet while we can easily recognize central instances of, say, subversive writing, we are also likely to encounter borderline cases with respect to which a more or less arbitrary decision may have to be made from time to time. However, faced with the colour called cyan, someone may demand that we tell them whether cyan is a kind of blue or a kind of green; forced to plump for one category or the other, we could do so, but we would still be aware of an essential arbitrariness to our allocation and also accept without question that our decision one way or the other has no consequences for straightforward cases of blue or green.

It would be interesting to consider why, with respect to certain freedoms, it should be felt, as it often seems to be, that a borderline case has an important bearing on a concept as a whole. Why should an exaggerated and possibly improper use of libel laws (as an intimidatory device, for example, to ensure silence) throw into question the general area of libel and even the very idea of it? Why should a misapplication of official secrets legislation seem to demand a complete overhaul of the Official Secrets Acts and provoke calls from some people for complete freedom of information?

The solution to these apparently conceptual problems rests in treating them as involving questions that are less philosophical than social, as I intend to show below. I need only point out now that the type of treatment given to borderline cases connected with freedom of expression and, for that matter, other liberties can be substantially different to that accorded other kinds of borderline case. With the latter the question is resolved either by recognizing that the problem must be permanently a borderline one as, for example, when we agree that cyan is in the end a kind of blue but continue to maintain that it is still very close to being a kind of green, or when we accept that we must have recourse to an arbitrary decision in individual cases, as in matters of taxation, where schemes are proposed to remove anomalies but not to abolish taxation altogether. Some social concepts, however, are typically not treated in this fashion at the present time, and therefore present us with a special kind of borderline case of which an individual account must be given.

Conceptual Uncertainty

Many contemporrary attitudes towards freedom of expression and its restriction do not result from logical, conceptual or rational considerations that arbitrary and anomalous decisions in borderline cases require a concept to be substantively revised or altogether abandoned; rather they are the corollary of social attitudes towards a concept arising independently of any anomalies. Borderline cases, far from being somehow objectionable in themselves, need to be thought of from both a philosophical and a practical point of view as a useful buffer-zone—and not the start of a slippery slope—protecting a concept like obscenity and subversiveness in its main functional areas.

Borderline cases for the application of a concept will therefore tend to arise anew when there is a shift in social attitudes. Seemingly arbitrary applications of censorship occur when censorship in a particular field is, because of its dependence on social attitudes, uncertain, on the wane, or suffering strong opposition, when a particular concept is undergoing a radical change or a shift in emphasis, or losing any connotation of disapproval it may have previously carried. (They will also occur, conversely, when because of a change in attitudes, restrictions in a certain area are growing; but for the most part the problem of censorship today has been—until the advent of the internet—tied to the phenomenon of declining and weakening restrictions.)

Cases of arbitrary action which have come about for these reasons may often be mistaken for genuinely conceptual borderline cases, which they are not. Obscenity, for example, has as a concept been noticeably weakened and narrowed, both in matters of law and in the eyes of many ordinary people, in its connection with sexual themes; but, interestingly, it is receiving wider and more intensive use with respect to violence and more unlikely themes such as income and wealth. Almost without question, in central cases at least, we regard libel and slander as one of the few properly justified bases for checks on free expression; and they too create problem cases because part of their area is shrinking, as in the matter of comment on public figures, particularly in the United States, while at the same time people who are increasingly concerned for their privacy demand measures which are close to censorship in effect in order to keep their personal lives hidden from the public gaze.

Censorship and Its Accord with the Nature of Society

Previous discussion about the arbitrary nature of censorship has turned on the practical realization of policy. It is clear that censorship can be contingently arbitrary. But is it more than contingently so? Two reasons may be put forward for believing that it may be necessarily arbitrary, or arbitrary in principle. First, no principle of censorship can be in complete accord with the nature of society in which it is found; second, in the framing of laws it is necessary to make explicit the bounds within which any law of censorship is to apply.

Even when fully approved in principle by all or most of the members of the society in which it has force, no censorship law will be in exact accord with all their wishes in every instance. This follows from an understanding of processes of social change. On the whole, the law is notoriously conservative, and perhaps has to be, lagging for the most part somewhat behind public opinion. Occasionally the law may be ahead of its time, notably when it is used as an instrument to effect a change in public opinion or to speed up a development of social attitudes that has already been initiated. In neither case do the applications of law and social behaviour and attitudes change simultaneously. Either the law brings about a change in behaviour or behaviour brings about a change in the law; the nature of this type of causal relationship requires that the two be out of step, however marginally. If law is intended to reflect majority social opinion as closely as possible, change in society and corresponding change in the law may be closely associated, but they can only rarely and coincidentally be simultaneous processes.

Censorship, bound up as it is with social ideas that are almost always in a greater or lesser state of flux, is fairly certain to be applied to a somewhat greater or somewhat smaller degree than it ought to be in the eyes of many people. This is the best state of affairs that can be aspired to, simply because of what society is like. In many cases the situation may be at some remove from the ideal: a censorship law, like any other law, may badly misjudge public opinion or completely disregard it. Such censorship need not be arbitrary in itself. Its principle may be internally consistent; but it will appear arbitrary to most of those affected by it. But however near to the perfection of the ideal a law may be, it will in some of its applications be at that moment out of step with public opinion, and if the decision is thought not to be mistaken in a specific case, it must still on that occasion appear to be an arbitrary one.

The Constraint of the Limiting Specifications of a Law

The consideration that any principle of censorship is going to be limited to a specific type of subject-matter or a specific mode of expression brings the discussion back to the problem of the borderline case. The nature of human opinions and values, of human ideas and their linguistic expression means that borderline cases are inevitable. Previously, borderline cases were considered as contingencies arising in the practice of censorship. It must now be admitted that borderline cases are always going to be met with as necessary features of censorship; they present a problem that can never be finally resolved. Creative work, critical work, intellectual work can never be compartmentalized or segregated off into discrete categories. The ways in which ideas are expressed and the content of those ideas themselves form a continuum. If we wish to alter or suppress any part of this range of expression it will be found that at the limits of our action, no matter where we decide to place those limits, we are obliged to behave in a necessarily arbitrary way, permitting some problem cases and prohibiting others. (If, faced with what presented themselves initially to us as problem cases, we were to decide them *all* in the same way, we should find new problem cases arising on their periphery.) Between those cases which just manage to be permitted and those which are hapless enough to be included within the margin of some prohibition there will not seem to be any substantive difference which would fairly justify our discrimination between the two. On account of its social aims and origins the justification of censorship is necessarily in terms of open-textured concepts, concepts that are 'blurred at the edges'; and by their nature such concepts lead us unavoidably into a position where in borderline cases we have to make arbitrary or *ad hoc* decisions.

Censorship is tied to open-textured valuational concepts and therefore, in certain cases, to an inevitable arbitrariness. It is just because of the concepts involved—obscenity, blasphemy, subversiveness, and so forth—that the instances of arbitrary practical action encountered cannot be avoided; and since they cannot be avoided we can hardly disapprove or despair of them but must come to terms with them. They are a necessary consequence of the ways in which we structure our lives conceptually. On occasion censorship is obliged to be carried out in an arbitrary fashion, but when it is arbitrary in this way it is not unfairly or unacceptably so. The arbitrariness inherent in possibly acceptable censorship must be distinguished from an unacceptable arbitrary practice of censorship.

An Interim Assessment

Censorship clearly is not without its failings in theory and to an even greater extent in practice. Our final judgment may be that no matter how perfect its realization censorship is by its very nature an unacceptable form of control in any society except in the most exceptional circumstances. Yet, in discussing censorship in principle, it is surely incumbent on the critic to disregard purely practical failings so long as they remain unconnected with theoretical necessities. All systems of control are far from the ideal in their execution but they may nevertheless have to be used. Given their usefulness and, in some cases, indispensability, it is fair when considering only the idea of controls to postulate the optimum conditions for their actual exercise.

What is to be said of the inherent weaknesses of censorship in principle? The only substantial criticism so far, as I hope I have shown, is the unfairness that may be visited on the borderline case. However, if certain areas of our lives are to be protected then, for reasons resulting from the logic of our concepts, borderline cases are inevitable. The consequent unfairness, in any case, is quite similar to that found in many areas, and many of them far removed from censorship and restrictions of freedom. If control of free speech is required, such unfairness has to be accepted, though its occcasions are to be lamented and avoided as far as possible.

Some questions still remain to be answered. Is censorship, or wider control of free speech, necessary? Are there values which compete with, or pre-empt, the values of freedom of expression, information and communication, or is free speech a supreme value?[19]

Paternalism, Interference and Human Dignity

In this section I want to look at another argument against censorship, which asserts that it is offensive to human dignity, inasmuch as the idea that they should be supervised and controlled in such a fashion is—or ought to be—found objectionable by mature adults who are citizens of a supposedly liberal-democratic society.[20] This argument conceives of censors as governors over, or guardians of, ordinary people; in certain respects, therefore, the latter are given the status of children.[21] For the ordinary citizen censorship becomes a mark of immaturity or servitude. For the modern liberal or democrat restrictions on freedom of expression are typically not to be counted among the permissible powers of the state, 'those that citizens could recognize while still regarding themselves as equal, autonomous, rational agents'.[22]

Adults exercise controls amounting to censorship on children. What they do in this regard is almost universally recognized to be valid and right in principle. This application of restrictions is endorsed by virtually all adults in society as necessary in the light of their purposes. It is true that some people may contend that even schoolchildren are *unduly* restricted and are wrongly denied access to some areas of knowledge and opinion, but they allow nevertheless that a veil must be drawn over discussion of some topics until *some* point in a child's development, however early that may be. Just where the line ought to be drawn for children is not a problem to be solved here; wherever the line is drawn, on one point there is no dispute in modern Western societies: that is, whether or not older children should be treated more like adults than like younger children, most assuredly adults should be treated as adults and not as children at all. Adults should not be subjected to the type of educational restrictions and controls similar to those imposed on children; and it seems that censorship is just such a control. By effectively treating mature adults like children any policy of censorship suggests that those in authority are contemptuous of that dignity which is properly accorded to the adult citizen.

If the foundations of education and censorship are regarded alike as requiring the idea of *direction*, the claim that censorship conflicts with human dignity would have to be regarded as correct. However, all education does not take a directive form, and it can be argued that little should do. If we think of education as involving guidance rather than direction, or advice rather than command, the type of educational controls and restrictions to which censorship is closest could be described simply as paternalistic. Despite the etymology of 'paternalism' and related words, to treat an adult as a child and to treat him or her paternalistically are not synonymous expressions; the first seems to involve a blatant affront to a person in a way in which the second does not. Here, for the sake of argument, it is fair to consider the combination of education and censorship in the least unfavourable way, and regard the educational features with which we are concerned as paternalistic. The particular question to be considered at this point is whether paternalism directed towards adults is truly an affront to their dignity.

The state, certainly, has legislated a wide range of measures which are largely paternalistic in both their intent and effect or which represent a kind of interference by authority with the individual's more or less private affairs that is very closely allied to paternalism. Positive measures to enhance the welfare of those in a degree of serious need not only restrict the freedom of those who are not in need (by imposing financial restraints in the form of taxes, for example) but may also eventually create the institutions of a social structure which markedly limits the freedom of everyone. (It may become necessary for a private health sector to be virtually abolished in order that the public health service is not deprived of needed medical staff, or for private education to be seriously constrained in order that the social ideals of public comprehensive education are not compromised.) Socialist measures lead through interference with individual action to an implied paternalistic direction of all members of society, even though paternalistic intentions are not present in the initial changes.

Nevertheless, although state control of education and medicine, together with other areas of social life, may be detrimental to certain types of freedom, there are few claims that it offends human dignity; it would be claimed rather that measures such as those relating to health, safety or education especially advance it. It cannot be argued that censorship offends human dignity *because* it is paternalistic or, more explicitly, *because* it is an instrument of supervision, guidance or control. If it is rejoined that censorship involves supervision and guidance in inappropriate areas where individual judgment can suitably be exercised and should be, it may be submitted in reply that interference by the state today often involves matters which require no expert knowledge and could fairly be left to the ordinary judgment of most people; in many matters people may properly make up their own minds about future courses of action, following their own good sense without interference from others.

Perhaps censorship offends human dignity not because it makes of a governing authority a paternalistic guardian, but because it involves not simply supervision, not even surveillance alone of a person, but quite often his being spied on by agents of the government or some organization. For censorship to be effective a government may require the opening of personal mail, the searching of offices, academic institutions and private residences, and the use of informers. The affront to a person's dignity here seems to present a more clear-cut case since such practices occasion invasions of privacy.

However, two functions of censorship must be distinguished: there is the censorship that exists to protect the public at large from exposure to pernicious ideas and opinions, and there is the censorship that exists to protect national security. Here the discussion is about what is largely a matter of moral, political, religious, intellectual or cultural censorship. This censorship is concerned with the expression, transmission and acquisition of ideas. Censorship in the interests of national security, on the other hand, is concerned with the communication of concrete items of information of a very practical importance in their own right. With regard to the transmission and dissemination of ideas the appropriate authority, where there is the legal possibility of censorship, may step in before or after publication, but there is little need for any kind of surreptitious surveillance. Surreptitious acts may appear to be part of a policy of censorship, but they belong more to a wider scheme of control than to censorship itself. In matters of national security different, pragmatic, considerations come into play, and indeed censorship assumes a very subordinate role as one instrument among others for the protection of the state. The rights and wrongs of censorship merge with the rights and wrongs of the security programme as a whole.

Later it may become evident that these two functions of censorship are not to be so easily distinguished. Lord Devlin remarked that 'there is disintegration when no common morality is observed, and history shows that the loosening of moral bonds is often the first stage of disintegration, so that society is justified in taking the same steps to preserve its moral code as it does to preserve its government and other essential institutions'.[23] The final result of a military attack by an external enemy and the result of the more insidious attack by moral or political corruption may be the same: the collapse and destruction of society. The division between the two kinds of attack is not always clearly to be seen; the line between the two may be blurred and uncertain. Especially in political censorship there is often a meeting between questions of physical security and questions about what is morally or culturally proper and acceptable to a society and its members. Communism, for example, was often presented as an insidious moral threat to free culture in the West, which, as such a threat, would also undermine national security and render the states of the West physically vulnerable to the enemy. For many, it seemed to pose the danger of a cultural 'fifth column' as an adjunct to the direct military threat.

Nevertheless, the two functions of censorship can be distinguished initially. Security measures can certainly lead to affronts to human dignity; but if censorship as a security measure is such an affront, and insofar as it is, it will form part of the general problem of restricting liberty in the interests of the preservation of the state and not part of the problem of censorship alone. Censorship as a policy in its own right exists primarily to protect society from pernicious ideas and ensure positive social development along certain lines. In this capacity it need not affront human dignity by its adoption of unacceptable techniques of surveillance. Nor need adult persons consider themselves to be specially offended by paternalistic measures that are not in fact exclusive in their paternalism to censorship.

I do not believe that certain types of censorship affront the dignity of adults. But if this assertion is to be accepted it depends on the reader's attitude to two other problems. One is the nature of formative education and the place in it of censorship and other restrictive measures, and also the difference between the education of children and that of adults—especially now that there is so much talk of 'lifelong learning'. The other concerns the significance of paternalistic intentions in the limiting of free speech and the possible distinction of restrictive measures of this kind from those in other areas.

The attitude which is adopted towards the second problem will be closely linked to that taken towards the first. If it is decided that education of adults may be formative in an essentially similar way to that in which the education of children is formative, then restrictions of a like kind will be as necessary in one as in the other; and paternalism will be as acceptable or unacceptable in relation to interference with free speech as it is in relation to social welfare and other areas of current state action. Again, all these arguments will depend on a specific conception of the nature of society. It is on the idea of a society and social benefits, and the significance of free speech in this respect, that the last major criticism of censorship centres.

The Social Benefits of Free Speech

Many of those who have argued for freedom of speech to be as extensive as possible have maintained that the unhindered expression of diverse opinions is vital to the health of democracy and works to the general benefit of society, and indeed of humanity, as a whole. Nevertheless, free speech is not finally justified by consequentialist arguments; to remain inviolate, it has to be a good in itself. Even if (impossibly) we should attain absolute certainty about the falsity of some opinion, 'stifling it would be an evil still', as Mill, who remains still the best exponent of the classical argument for free speech, put it.[24]

If such is truly the case then we must be indifferent to the truth or falsehood, real or perceived, of an opinion or idea and equally, by extension, to whatever worth, goodness or rightness an opinion or an action seems intrinsically to lack. By permitting wrong opinions as well as right ones we benefit by gaining 'the clearer perception and livelier impression of truth, produced by its collision with error';[25] through the suppression of free discussion, according to Mill, 'the great harm done is to those who are not heretics, and whose whole mental development is cramped, and their reason cowed, by the fear of heresy'.[26] Again, 'teachers and learners go to sleep at their post, as soon as there is no enemy in the field'.[27] Mill's points are reminiscent of Milton's argument to the same effect: 'Our Faith and Knowledge thrives by exercise as well as our limbs and complexion.'[28] Interestingly, despite ostensible appeals to the intrinsic value of freedom and free speech in particular, the words of both Mill and Milton constantly threaten a lapse into consequentialism and the conclusion that the positive valuation of free speech and the negative valuation of censorship really depend on their results.

The argument is that the permitting of all forms of actual or supposed error (so long as they do not present some immediate real danger to others of a mostly physical kind) is generally beneficial: the truth is more emphatically brought out and realized by those who subscribe to it, our intellectual and reasoning powers are sharpened and developed, and society itself is better off because dissenting minorities almost always have something worthwhile to contribute to our social and intellectual development, if only by contrast, even when they are mostly in the wrong. George Bernard Shaw's words tie this approach up well and emphasize its implications by taking it to an extreme: 'an overwhelming case can be made out for the statement that no nation can prosper or even continue to exist without heretics and advocates of shockingly immoral doctrines.'[29] As a corollary we may note that we are encouraged in the West to prefer pluralism on mixed grounds which combine intrinsic value and consequentialist benefit.[30]

Some Qualifications

The positive side of the argument here is that exposure to error develops and strengthens our intellectual and rational powers. So it may. But there are two points I think it worthwhile to make here. First, restrictions on freedom of expression have in practice rarely been such as to prohibit knowledge of specific opinions or information to everyone in society. George Orwell in his novel *Nineteen Eighty-four* portrayed a society where not only had the record of much knowledge and opinion been destroyed but also language itself was in the process of being modified so as to render it impossible even to think along prohibited lines. In the real world, however, where censorship has been systematically practised, knowledge of banned opinions, beliefs and ideas has been available to at least some of those who have been making a genuine inquiry about them, and human nature is such that only seldom have 'erroneous' publications, for example, been completely extirpated. The western love of written records is too strong. Following instincts of human nature, perhaps, the authorities seem unable usually to destroy materials completely even when access is to all intents not allowed, as with the contents of the old 'Private Case' in the British Museum or of politically sensitive files kept beyond the normal release date of thirty years (in the United Kingdom) bears witness.

Censorship is usually directed towards the mass of the people, and a select number of individuals are excluded from its application. The consequence is that this limited availability guards against the possibility that the survival of some valuable knowledge or opinion will be placed in real jeopardy. Criticism about social benefits need not bear so strongly on a system of partial or differential censorship. For those who are allowed access to otherwise forbidden knowledge and opinion the benefits of unrestricted access—the enrichment and strengthening of their thought—must presumably remain. At least indirectly, therefore, the benefits are potentially still available to their society in the future, if not at present. In the most free societies, after all, few people have direct access to information and opinion, even though they have the right to it, and obtain most of their knowledge and opinion through the mediation of some authority or expert. The argument requires that the whole range of opinions and ideas should be taken up by *anyone* interested in order that his or her intellectual and spritual life may be developed through the exercise of mental powers and critical judgment.

The second point of importance is contained in the aside above, that with regard to not only most of our knowledge but also most of our opinion we are all uncritically dependent on secondary sources of one kind or another. This is freely acknowledged to be the case with our factual knowledge. In view of such dependence would we have much hesitation in allowing the legitimacy of a ban (or of a demand for specific textual editing) on popular and influential books which deliberately or negligently distorted or falsified in a flagrant way the basic facts of history, physics or geography, on books which purposely misinformed or misled? Would it not be socially irresponsible if those entrusted with authority did not take action? The question has only recently resurfaced as one to be asked in connection with the publication of historical works denying the Holocaust. Ought we to consider opinions to be so different? Most of them are acquired by us in a secondary way from social sources of one kind or another. Indeed, there is a significant body of opinion which wants to give effect to 'political correctness' by banning or rewriting works, particularly for children, which express unwelcome (incorrect) social attitudes. It is easy for the two senses of 'correctness' (factual truth and moral or social desirability) to become fused.

If there is a social responsibility to be practised as well as preached, there are the makings of a case for the recognition of those who in a social or institutional role are the sources or mediators of those opinions and who act in good faith for the preservation of those values which seem to be of social importance. Today, philosophical opinion as well as more general social attitudes are on the whole against so-called elitism and particularly against it with regard to ethical matters. If a case can be made in support of expert judgments about social aims, if it is possible to support the thesis that some people are more qualified than others to judge questions of value, morality or literary and artistic merit, then a foundation is laid for the principle of censorship.

The social benefits of free speech must also be set against the importance of social cohesion and allowing society to develop in a guided manner along certain lines. Free discussion is not the only means of strengthening ideas and beliefs. Indeed, it would seem to be less of a way of immediately confirming true knowledge or right belief than of allowing different systems, incorporating different scales of values, to compete with each other indiscriminately, even though the best might win through in the long run. Is it possible to have a single conception of a proper society? Is there to be one system of values in a society to determine each area of its members' lives, or are there to be different and competing values? How justified is a homogeneous society in attempting to protect itself from being transformed into a heterogeneous one?

A Weakness in the Argument for Free Speech

Even for a pluralist society there is a weakness in the argument about the social benefits brought by free speech. Incorporated in the argument for universal open access to all manner of opinions there is a variant of the mistaken empirical assumption that in a free situation the true opinion will be, or is overwhelmingly likely to be, preferred to the false opinion (and I have already discussed this mistaken belief). In this final argument we are presented with a related claim, that we can afford to expose ourselves to all kinds of opinions because, if the truth is established and generally accepted by the individual members of a society, we need not fear that it will ever succumb to falsehood or error—as if, to recall Milton's imagery, physical exercise always can *only* strengthen the body and never lead, for example, to a fatal heart attack.

This is not the case. Free opinion may work as easily to the disadvantage of a society as to its advantage. A beneficial outcome is not guaranteed by the most well-meaning of intentions. I cannot believe that it is always true that a reasonably unbounded toleration of free opinion and expression will at the worst leave us none the poorer. By allowing complete freedom of expression we create the prospect of an unknown loss as well as an unknown gain; we place those truths and proper values that we do possess seriously at risk. We may think it worthwhile to take this risk, but we must be conscious that there is a risk involved and not believe that there is everything to gain and nothing to lose. Whether or not we believe that the free expression of opinions and the unrestricted dissemination of knowledge should be permitted, we must constantly be on our guard, for truth demands continuous vigilance: to be preserved, it must be guarded and cherished. The events of history have too often contradicted the assumptions of an optimistic rationalism.

Looking Forward

My discussion of criticisms of censorship in the foregoing chapters has been intended to produce a better realization of the proper place of truth in a society and the dangers that threaten it. The last criticism should make us more aware of larger questions concerning the importance of a secure social order and its preservation. To these questions I shall return for a fuller discussion, particularly in the context of the significance of censorship for a homogeneous society and its continued survival. It will be seen that there the pluralistic possibilities created by freedom of speech may be socially destructive, even when they make a positive contribution to the enhancement of a value like that of truth.

The following chapters invite the reader to consider the connections of free speech with some of its possible justifications. I introduce these by way of a discussion of education; this brings up one aspect of the problem of the relation between society and its members, which is manifested in the ways in which the state treats its citizens and, conversely, the attitude which citizens have towards their state and its government.

Notes

1 John Milton, *Areopagitica*, reprinted in *Complete Prose Works* (New York and London, 1953), Vol. II, p. 561.

2 In *Abrams* v *United States*, 250 U.S. 616 (1919), quoted in Jerome Barron, *Freedom of the Press for Whom?* (Indianapolis, 1973), p. 320.

3 This really amounts to nothing more than a coherence theory of truth. Its latest exponent is Richard Rorty, in his *Philosophy and the Mirror of Nature* (Oxford, 1979) and other writings.

4 Schauer, *op. cit.*, p. 16.

5 *Principles of Politics*, extracted in John Plamenatz (ed.), *Readings from Liberal Writers* (London, 1965), p. 187.

6 See John Stuart Mill, *On Liberty* (Harmondsworth, 1974), p. 77.

7 *Ibid.*, pp. 78–79.

8 *Ibid.*, p. 79.

9 *Ibid.*

10 *Ibid.*

11 It should be emphasized that regarding restrictions on freedom this argument runs fully counter to Mill's position in *On Liberty*.

12 It is worth noting that where press censorship has been practised it has sometimes been the case that newspapers have not been allowed to appear with the blank spaces where the censored material has been removed; this is presumably in the vain hope that intelligent readers (and perhaps not so intelligent ones) can remain unaware that any censorship has taken place.

13 See below, chapter 4.

14 See below, chapter 4. The resolution of a practical problem through the use of restrictions will be directed by certain evaluative presuppositions typifying a social culture.

15 J.B. Bury refers to 'arbitrary prohibitions or barriers' in his book *A History of Freedom of Thought* (London, 1913), p. 18. On capriciousness, see further, David Tribe, *Questions of Censorship* (London, 1973), chapter 9, 'What you can get away with'.

16 There is an analogy here with the way in which some opponents of capital punishment in the United States hold that this form of punishment is (in constitutional terms) 'cruel and unusual' intrinsically and not just in the manner in which it is legislated for or given effect. The Supreme Court, of course, has decided that capital punishment is only contingently cruel and unusual and the defects in its implementation as a policy can be remedied.

17 The lack of belief in moral and many other kinds of evaluative expertise results from a scepticism about sets of standards; it does not arise from doubt that there may exist degrees of proficiency in understanding and working with one accepted scheme of values.

18 On the significance of this idea for law, see the now classic discussion by H.L.A. Hart in *The Concept of Law* (Oxford, 1961), chapter 7.

19 If free speech is not a supreme value in itself it may be an inescapable consequence of adherence to some such value. Thus freedom of speech and liberty of thought are 'required by the first principle of justice' (John Rawls, *A Theory of Justice* (Oxford, 1972), p. 225).

20 *Cf.* Maurice Cranston, *What are Human Rights?* (London, 1973), p. 38.

21 *Cf. ibid.*, p. 40.

22 T. Scanlon, 'A theory of freedom of expression', *Philosophy and Public Affairs*, 1 (1971–72), p. 215.

23 Devlin, *op. cit.*, p. 13.

24 Mill, *op. cit.*, p. 77.

25 *Ibid.*, p. 76.

26 *Ibid.*, p. 95.

27 *Ibid.*, p. 105.

28 Milton, *op. cit.*, vol. II, p. 543.

29 Quoted in O'Higgins, *op. cit.*, p. 155.

30 Whether a pluralist society is preferable on a purely consequentialist assessment looks like a problem to be settled through empirical research. However, evaluating the advantages and disadvantages of different kinds of society depends on a weighting of values which is already partially determined by the researcher's own sociological context.

3 Philosophical Connections

The Restrictions of Education

To the young we deny unhindered access to opinion, knowledge and information of any kind. Discussion of censorship should find it useful, I believe, to consider the rationale of the restrictions found in education. The bringing up of children is an area of social life where both extensive restrictions and directed guidance play an unquestioned part. In the widest sense the educational process includes not only a denial of certain things to children but also the positive encouragement of the maturing child to adopt (in a pluralist society) one among several socially approved forms of opinion, belief and knowledge.

The interests of a proper upbringing therefore require the practice of certain measures of censorship. Children are not to be permitted access to some kinds of books, magazines, films and other published material (now including, of course, websites on the internet). It is not thought proper for them to take part with adults in discussions of some matters, and not just on the ground of their lack of knowledge. Indeed, younger children are not supposed to know very much about certain subjects, particularly sexual ones. Knowledge of several kinds, especially about different systems of morals and religion is typically limited, if available at all, in formal educational situations.

For even the staunchest believers in liberty some restrictions are not merely permissible but required in a person's minority. Mill took it for granted that society should have 'absolute power' over children during 'the whole period of childhood and nonage' in order to 'make them capable of rational conduct in life'.[1] It is the possibility of a fairly intensive upbringing of children in the right conduct of life that justifies the later complete freedom of adults. Mill nowhere doubted his belief that children should occupy this subordinate and unfree position; and the purpose behind the prohibition is evident: enforcing restrictions on children promotes the development of certain capacities along socially and intellectually desirable lines. We thus make them capable of what society considers rational conduct. Even today, although the educational situation is undoubtedly a more liberal one than obtained in Victorian times and arguably, in some respects, a more liberal one than Mill could have imagined, the belief that children up to a certain age should suffer marked limitations of their liberty in the cause of their general upbringing is almost univerally held. There may be disputes about just where the line should be drawn, both regarding the age at which it is most aptly to be drawn and regarding exactly what matters should be excluded from a child's unfettered curiosity. But there is no dispute that some substantial portion of a child's life is to be passed before that line is reached and that some subjects require careful treatment in the child's interests. Those who believe sex of less importance, for example, often argue that children should not be exposed to violence as entertainment.

The commonly held liberal position—although still to be fully realized in many professedly liberal societies—is markedly different respecting the educational position of adults. Here, in short, freedom of expression and information is ideally to be given the widest possible bounds, albeit a few limits have to remain, and access to all kinds of factual information and moral and political opinion is to be as unhindered as possible. But we must always remember that for the classic liberal thinkers this freedom was to be allowed to those who had, ideally, been educated according to the norms of a 'civilized' society.

Child and Adult

For the liberal there is a sharp distinction between child and adult. In the life of every person of sound mind there comes a point when he assumes not only the adult's responsibilities but also his freedoms. How is the placing of that point to be justified, when the law, on behalf of society, determines it so arbitrarily to be identically the same for everybody? The focus of attention here is not to be on children, for restrictions on them are not questioned in principle. The need rather is to examine how we are to justify educational restrictions and the significance that our justification has for beliefs about an adult's right to free speech and free inquiry.

If children are in some ways denied freedom of information this restriction is enforced not because of some arbitrary attitude towards certain ages, or some purely formal educational requirement, but because of some truly substantive concern about their characters and personalities and our opinion of, and feelings about, their mental and moral development. In sum, we do not feel that they are yet capable of exercising mature and rational judgment. If children are treated as such for a reason of substance the criterion of age should surely be used as a general guideline and by no means as a *strict* indication of when restrictive education should cease and a full adult liberty be granted. Following a substantive criterion, the granting of full freedom of choice in moral, religious and political matters would be dependent properly on each individual's character and mental development. The explicit age of adulthood would not be a universal rule but a flexible norm. If, for example, such a norm of full age were eighteen, then full freedom might be granted to a precocious few at fourteen or fifteen, to many or most at around eighteen, to some at twenty, or twenty-five, or thirty, and to a few individuals very late in life or never. This sort of approach is not unknown even in the rigidly formal context of a court of law, where the evidence of children, if pertinent, will be deemed admissible, and assessed on a case-by-case basis depending on the court's judgment of a particular child's intellectual capacity.

Few of us would want to adopt the inverse position, disallowing the rights of adulthood to people who seemed to fail the test of showing that they deserved them. James Stephen, Mill's intellectual opponent, recognized the problem raised here. He argued against Mill's way of thinking, which created a sharp qualitative distinction between the child and the adult, by pointing out that it assumes that it is absolute, whereas 'minority and majority are questions of degree, and the line which separates them is arbitrary'.[2] He asked how society, having accepted the position of the moral educator of children and having educated children up to a certain point, can 'draw a line at which education ends and perfect moral indifference begins'.[3] According to this argument society draws a line between child and adult at an arbitrary age, disregarding the evident differences in development that there are between one person and another.

We need to draw a line in law to distinguish between categories of persons, even though not all people clearly fall on one side of the line or the other when we consider why we are drawing the line. Age is a very convenient way of making distinctions objective, but the very ease with which we can apply it serves to emphasize its arbitrary character. If it is in truth ultimately arbitrary the best justifications (beyond operational practicality) for a legal age of majority and its concomitant restrictions on minors are two. First, a fixed age fairly represents a kind of average point at which people are adult in character according to current general opinions in society. Second, the real purpose of educational restrictions is not to create some fully-formed opinions and beliefs, but to make a foundation within the individual for what society believes to be the right sorts of attitudes, in recognition of the probability that to form opinions completely and universally would be a virtually impossible task and that, in any case, to overdetermine them would really be to the detriment of society.

That educational restrictions on freedom of information contribute towards an individual's 'start in life' seems a reasonable enough statement. They set that person on the right road, as society sees it, but beyond a certain stage in life they ideally impose no obligation to continue along this road. Their education as children is like a map which eventually accompanies adults as a guide to the broad features of social life but which does not coerce them into taking any particular direction or confine them to discovering no more than those details already indicated on it. This interpretation is exemplified in the assertion that restrictions are imposed on children for the better development of their 'potentiality for choice'.[4] It will be pointed out shortly that it is unacceptable.

We might make even more sense of the age-limit by adopting the stance of the educator. In one way its arbitrariness could be eliminated if we were to look at an age such as sixteen, eighteen or twenty-one from the point of view not of learning but of teaching. Eighteen would be not the age at which the individual is considered to have taken in sufficient knowledge of the world and to have been sufficiently acculturated morally and socially but rather the age at which society believes it has had enough time to impart to that person adequate instruction in such opinion and to effect sufficient development of his or her rationality. This is Mill's point. Implicit in this view seems to be the position that what the individual has made of the instruction is to be accounted less important than the act of instruction itself: it suffices merely that instruction should be given.

To centre education in this way on the instructor and the act of instruction rather than on the child and the assimilation of the instruction is, surely, curious; what matters is that instruction should be effectively taken up, not just that it should be given. Restrictions are imposed not simply to provide an *opportunity* for favourable development but to affect the actual course and content of that development. They are imposed in the name of education because it is generally believed in society that a certain standard ought to be reached and is presumably capable of being reached by the ordinary person. This standard is not a merely formal one, to be defined in terms of the development of a child's abilities or his potentiality for choice. The educational purpose of restrictions is a rather more substantive one than such phrases suggest. Education is not concerned with the mere form of a child's future adult behaviour—the widest ability to make choices—it is also very much concerned with the content, from which springs the ability to make the choice that is right. More, it intends not only that members of society will know what the right choices are and have the capacity to make them but also that they will in fact make those choices for themselves. Mill, too, was making a rather stronger point than we might think when he wrote of making individuals 'capable of rational conduct in life', for developed rationality will at best allow only a very limited range of choices and in many cases no choice at all; education is a matter of teaching children what they are to understand as the single type of rational behaviour.

The Requirements of Society

A certain approved level and content of opinion is clearly, if tacitly, required by society; and it is expected that these will be developed in the average person. Restrictions demonstrate that education in part must conform to certain preadopted attitudes and that associated instruction is intended to be assimilated permanently. Neither society as a whole nor any responsible adult believes in complete freedom in the educational process, expressly ruling out of the lives of young children pornography, blasphemy, the advocacy of violence of an antisocial kind (but by no means all violence), and the explicit teaching of antisocial behaviour generally. It is no kind of logical requirement that certain possibilities are excluded, but a contingent one. Attitudes relating to education derive from established social values. The assumptions underlying education are not self-evident; on the contrary, they constitute part of the social framework and their functional consequences (consciously apprehended or not) are to perpetuate this form of society or at least ensure the continued existence of its most basic values and a directed, acceptable change.

The education of children's opinions has as its basis some assumptions generally undisputed, not by *most* members of society, but by *all* reasonable people. These assumptions embody attitudes relating to the limits of reasonable or rational possibilities for thought and behaviour. Their effective presence shows that even a liberal education is not intended to lead to a literally complete freedom of thought in the educated adult. In every society certain things (but not always the same things) are held up as 'wrong' from the very beginning of a person's life, and only the rarest and most independently minded individuals will later come to question the fundamental presuppositions which they share with other members of society—and even then they will do so only to a limited extent. From the pervasiveness of such restrictions on freedom of thought it must be concluded that in the interests of social life instruction is not simply carried out along certain lines but, more, is designed in order that the individual assimilate certain basic and very general approved attitudes. There must implicitly be an interest in what standards individuals actually reach in relevant areas; therefore the line of demarcation between the child and the adult cannot be intended to be an entirely arbitrary one. There is to be found a qualitative distinction constituted by the substantive development that should have been effected in individuals, by the time they reach adulthood, through their education.

The Problem of the Immature or Deviant Adult

Probably many people, including those in authority, believe that the age of adulthood represents the stage at which a satisfactory state of opinions and attitudes has been reached in most people through a proper upbringing. However, even under the most efficient educational service and in even the most harmonious social surroundings providing for informal education a few individuals will either fail or refuse to grasp the moral and social standards that are set them (and they will by no means generally be persons who should be institutionalized). Such people may form a numerous group, one about which society must have a serious concern. The proponents of continuing restrictions for adults would argue that they face up to this problem, albeit they conceive it on a wider scale, since they would claim that many or most adults have not reached the proper stage of development to be allowed unrestricted access in every area of knowledge and opinion. Even in a free society, where measures of censorship imposed on adults are minimal, the problem of the immature or deviant person has to be faced. If immaturity can be recognized, and if there are valid grounds for the treatment of more obviously immature people, what implications are suggested for the workings of society in general?

Educational restrictions, despite their intentions, produce different results in different people. That people have varying capacities for making use of the education they are given argues that, for reasons of some substance, education, including the use of restrictions, could profitably be carried on for some persons beyond the nominal age of adulthood. If social restrictions have substantive aims society ought to impose restrictions for the sake of consistency in its educational policy at all levels and stages in a person's development. Rather than adulthood being granted according to the arbitrary sign of a legal age, degrees of adulthood and maturity could be determined in more authentic ways. This would not necessarily be impracticable, although it might present complexities of administration, because the need to recognize abilities and qualifications is already present in many areas of life.

Education and Indoctrination

The idea that society could be seen as simply *offering* opinions through education must be rejected. Society attempts to inculcate opinions and attitudes into its future adult members for social purposes. Rousseau's dictum, in *Émile,* that in educating children the state's aim was to ensure that they become patriotic by inclination and instinct, was also, I suspect, Mill's vision of the ideal for rationality (if not for patriotism), albeit stated less frankly. These opinions which have been absorbed through their education will, it is hoped, be carried largely unmodified by adult citizens throughout their lives, and they will be conducive, it is believed, to the well-being and good order of the society in which they live. The objection may be made that the education of children is not, or properly ought not to be, directed to the inculcation of opinions or to indoctrination of any kind at all.

This objection can be dealt with briefly. It puts forward a distinction between teaching what the right choices are and indoctrinating individuals so that they will without question make those right choices. A common form of the argument is expressed in a comment like the following: 'We don't teach children opinions as such, but we do try to teach them how to make a proper choice for themselves later in life.' If in social matters we were dealing with ways of making decisions by logical deduction, such an ambition might well be feasible: it would be the teaching of an unopinioned method of choice. But this ambition is hardly practicable, or rather it is conceptually impossible in the real world. In the type of education in question we are very much caught up in the complex web of social values. To teach someone how to make a choice among values can only be to imply that one value is to be preferred to another; and to teach a *proper* choice and how to make it is to teach which values are to be preferred. To teach a proper choice is what the very minimum of the appropriate education must do, for, after all, anyone can make some sort of choice without instruction.

A related argument allows the inculcation of certain fundamental general attitudes in a free education while rejecting the indoctrination of detailed opinions and beliefs. Many people might believe that the allowing of freedom within the defined limits of the acceptable was equivalent to allowing a proper reasonable freedom. For example, it may be that no religious teaching involving specific doctrines is forced on the child; yet at the same time there is general religious instruction of a nondenominational but tendentious kind insofar as it is taught that the personal adoption of a religious system is preferable to possessing no religious beliefs at all (a point of view that perhaps can be advanced only by reluctant agnostics!). There is freedom here at the first level, allowing choice between religious beliefs, but not at the second level, which would allow complete rejection of all religion. However, the lack of freedom at the second level determines significantly some of the detailed content of first-level opinions and beliefs.

Children cannot be taught how to make 'proper' choices unless it is ensured that they adopt certain opinions to the exclusion of others. No kind of education can enable children to develop entirely within themselves criteria for proper choices, as if knowledge of right values was somehow innate or latent. Teaching cannot be seen in a Platonic way as a kind of midwife to a process of self-development. It is true that sometimes the values may already be there for the teacher to bring out and develop through formal education; but they still will have had an external origin which will be straightforwardly traceable to the social context and the type of the child's general upbringing.

Protection

Up to this point my discussion seems to have presupposed that virtually all restrictions applied to children and related to censorship are carried out for educational purposes. It might be argued that on the contrary many restrictions have as their primary purpose the protection of the individual child and that, further, most juvenile censorship and related restrictions have this purpose, being *typically* protective and not educational, although possibly possessing some educational benefit.

Against what might we be seeking to protect children by restricting what they are exposed to? The likely answer would be that children require protection against corruption, which is a real and present danger to them. This answer is correct, but it should be realized that corruption is not at all in the same sort of category as, say, bodily violence, against which, of course, protection is also necessary. Violence consists of a single discrete event; corruption is a lasting personality change, not (properly speaking) any actual immediate event, although that may be all that is needed in a few cases to bring about the change. Thus protection against violence and protection against corruption are not similar; they have different purposes. The first protects against an immediate occurrence; the second protects against a development which, although it may be brought about very occasionally by a single experience, is more likely to gain strength and mark an individual only through a succession of experiences. Ideally the argument would be that we protect children against corruption until such time as their character is developed enough to withstand it, as it should be later in life, much as we protect them against other assaults, not always of a physical kind, which adults can more readily resist. However, since protection is against a type of development rather than a single experience, the nature of the protection embodies certain developmental aims. Plainly protective measures are carried out to ensure proper development of the child's personality and thus to contribute to its development. By protecting a child against corruption we seek not merely to protect him against isolated events in his life but also to safeguard the development of his personality and encourage the progress of that development along certain approved lines.

Restrictions and Adults

My argument thus far has been that educational restrictions are directed towards a child's development and therefore have a certain aim. It has been assumed that some persons are accounted adults notwithstanding their failure to attain the desired standard in fields of moral and social behaviour as set by their education. Restrictions of freedom are enforced as a contribution to development, enabling the correct course to be more easily taken. The treatment of children seems to imply that freedom is a conditional right and that the stated age at which a child becomes an adult is fixed largely for the sake of convenience. Consideration of the aims that must lie behind education seem to tally with Stephen's way of thinking; in an ideal world restrictions would be appropriate to each person's stage of development. It is not itself the concept of freedom as a right which justifies the demand of adults for free speech and a general absence of censorship.

What justifies the absence of restrictions on adults? I have already explored the idea that under ideal conditions the individual can in some sense be deemed to be 'prepared' for life. But an additional consideration is that this position is supported by the principle of equality. Thereby, if one adult has the right to a certain freedom then all have. Just as children may not vote while all adults (with a few exceptions) may, so children are subjected to types of restrictions to which adults are not. Equality enables us to divorce the idea of restrictions based on an individual's age from any *central* connection with the need for the continual protection of the individual from harmful influences and the continuous educatinal development of his character. Equality, in our society, is not based on achievement or ability or related to character development; in that respect it is an absolute right.

What is the basis of the distinction between the child and the adult? Equality is not some incidental feature characterizing various aspects of social life but is itself one chief distinguishing feature of adulthood as opposed to childhood. When a person reaches adulthood he or she is to be treated as an equal. To the principle of equality the idea of actual maturity of judgment, except in the most extreme cases, is not to be considered relevant. Before the law the principle is one of equal responsibility, with only the insane absolved; for the franchise the principle is 'one person, one vote', with no property, literacy or intelligence requirements. Similarly, when it comes to the expression of opinion, specifically the freedom to speak and the freedom to listen, all people are equal; none should impose or be imposed on; each has an equal right to express himself in whatever way, and an equal right to have access to information or opinion. Although restrictions continue to exist, we believe that complete freedom of expression and inquiry, responsibly used, is the true ideal for all reasonable people. It is the principle of equality which provides the core of support for this belief.

Questions for a society aspiring to complete freedom of speech remain. How cogent a support for this freedom is the concept of equality? Ought other considerations to be borne in mind? If they ought, it must be remembered that to set about evaluating relative maturity in moral or political judgment is no easy task: indeed, it would have serious consequences throughout any liberal society, perhaps threatening the value of freedom in its most cherished areas. The disadvantages of too much freedom—the danger of pornography for morals and of racism for politics are two examples—might seem worth suffering to help preserve genuine intellectual freedom, the true freedom of reason.

Equality and Paternalism

When individuals become adults they are freed from the tutelage of their parents and, to some degree, of the state, and they acquire full responsibilities of their own. At the legal age of adulthood they become full citizens. For the law the essence of adulthood is self-responsibility; past a certain age people are presumed to be capable of looking after themselves. This point is now obscured by the presence in many countries of a welfare system which, despite many recent changes in the United Kingdom and elsewhere, is still extensive, together with many measures which involve interference with personal freedom and autonomy. Nevertheless, we assert that the principle of self-responsibility still holds, and that the state in theory provides only a safety-net to catch those who fall into some misfortune. In recent years the political imperative has been to impose a more restritive interpretation of what a 'safety-net' is. Indeed, for some people self-responsibility has been realized in a harsh way through the effective removal of a degree of welfare provision since the 1980s in the United Kingdom and elsewhere. Formally, responsibilities and self-responsibility presuppose equality. In consequence, all adults are to be deemed equally competent, with only occasional specified exceptions, of exercising responsibilities, of being held responsible legally and morally and, in principle, of looking after themselves.

Respecting the well-known distinction between numerical and proportional equality in the ordinary world of affairs today, there seems a noticeable tendency to confuse or conflate the two. Egalitarian forces appear to be taking us to a stage where proportional equality yields ever more ground to numerical equality, as has happened with the spread of universal suffrage in the twentieth century. Ability and knowledge seem increasingly discredited as criteria for marked differences of treatment or reward. For the freedom of information—the freedom to read and listen, for example—numerical equality has for some time been the guiding principle; no longer can a paterfamilias forbid his wife or servants to read a book which he could permit himself to read.[5] For the freedom of expression, however, the concept of proportional equality is probably more apt to contemporary circumstances, although superficial homage may be paid to the numerical kind. A person's access to some of the media of communication is plainly governed by, among other things, his education, competence, interests or appeal (as well as to criteria which have no connection with any conception of equality[6]), which, without doubt, are relevant to the practical realization of his freedom to use an effective medium to express himself publicly.

Equality of Judgment

The egalitarian argument against censorship seems to be that it is wrong for those in authority to impose their own opinions on others without allowing them to exercise their own judgment, even with respect to themselves, as they think fit. Censorship is a restriction of freedom, obviously enough, but in this connection one based on a belief that different persons do not have an equal capacity to exercise their judgment satisfactorily on their own behalf: the censors are more competent to exercise their judgment on other people's behalf than are those people themselves. The liberal argument is that as far as self-regarding actions are concerned, each person is quite free, absolutely—or certainly to the extent that every other person is free; personal freedom is based on the idea that all people are to be considered equal to exercise their own judgment about their own behaviour. Every competent adult is in principle morally independent.

This concept of the equal freedom of each person in this regard may perhaps be intimately linked with the Kantian idea of the respect which is owed equally to each person as a rational moral agent. If it is, the assertion that people should be free to exercise their own judgment on their own behalf is not an empirically based claim about the actual capacities of any specifiable real person but a metaphysical claim about each person's possession of a free and rational will. It is then a right of a person as such to exercise his or her own judgment in his or her own regard, with others having no right to impose their own judgment or to overrule that person's judgment in the moral area while actions remain self-regarding. The possession of this right is assessed without reference to actual abilities and is defeasible only by socially recognized incapacities such as mental disability.

I do not need to labour the criticisms of such a metaphysical position: they are obvious and well-known. As Bernard Williams has pointed out, 'it seems empty to say that all men are equal as moral agents, when the question, for instance, of men's responsibility for their actions is one to which empirical considerations are clearly relevant, and one which moreover receives answers in terms of different degrees of responsibility and different degrees of rational control over action'.[7] If it is really the case that people have varying capacities to exercise their judgment rightly or appropriately or usefully, how can a claim that they should all have an equal right to exercise their judgment in a certain class of cases be supported in a properly functioning society?

The argument for moral autonomy must cover in the end more than self-regarding actions. It must also extend to support of the individual's right to act in good faith reasonably and responsibly towards others and obey the dictates of conscience whenever that seems necessary. But perhaps the belief in people's capacities to exercise their own judgment may be more easily saved by confining that capacity (empirically) to self-regarding cases. I mention two problematical points at this juncture without further discussion. It is doubtful that there are many truly self-regarding actions, and perhaps there are no significant ones at all. Further, such a restriction of judgment to self-regarding actions would already be a serious curtailment of moral freedom.

The case for freedom and corresponding equality in the matter of self-regarding actions is clearly put by Mill; it remains so embedded in the foundation of our western democratic theory, if not its practice, that the relevant passage deserves to be quoted at length.

> Neither one person, nor any number of persons, is warranted in saying to another human creature of ripe years, that he shall not do with his life for his own benefit what he chooses to do with it. He is the person most interested in his own well-being: the interest which any other person, except in cases of strong personal attachment, can have in it, is trifling, compared with that which he himself has; the interest which society has in him individually (except as to his conduct to others) is fractional, and altogether indirect: while, with respect to his own feelings and circumstances, the most ordinary man or woman has means of knowledge immeasurably surpassing those that can be possessed by anyone else. ... Considerations to aid his judgment, exhortations to strengthen his will, may be offered to him, even obtruded on him, by others; but he himself is the final judge. All errors which he is likely to commit against advice and warning, are far outweighed by the evil of allowing others to constrain him to what they deem his good.[8]

This is the familiar argument against paternalism and related forms of interference. There are, of course, many different kinds of interference. Throughout the following discussion I make rather free use of the word 'paternalism', although—strictly speaking—not all of the interference to be subsumed under this word exemplifies true paternalism. Yet such different measures as compulsory education, provision of social security, and drug legislation are instituted by the state with aims that are at bottom very closely related. They have the intention of establishing and furthering a particular kind of society: equality and conformity are different aspects of the same social attitude. 'Paternalism' in a wide sense is intended to cover all the many different facets of interference in the interests of others—supervision, control, direction, etc.—or at least to stand for them by association. Here, this wide use of the word may be partly vindicated by etymological considerations (although these should always be employed with caution): a father, it has been traditionally thought, not only knows better than his children in many ways, helping them in their ignorance and being prepared to come to their assistance if they are in trouble of any kind, but he also forbids his children some things, controls their activities, directs and supervises their behaviour, and generally says how things are to be done, just in his capacity as a father.

By dint of its etymology, paternalism denies equality. The child is not the equal of its father. The basic principle of paternalism is that some do know better than others. This empirical claim is not one that is denied by egalitarians, of whom few, with the insight granted by twentieth-century psychology, would support Mill in his assertion that the ordinary person knows himself better than anyone else can. If some people know better than others, the anti-egalitarian may argue, they should be given the authority and power to protect, or compel, or act on behalf of, those who are less knowledgeable, less intelligent, less fortunate or even, perhaps, less inclined to engage in desirable activities. I believe it profitable to examine the arguments for paternalism in the most difficult cases for its supporters, namely self-regarding actions (with the assumption that there are at least a few such). It is in connection with these actions that the paternalist case must be weakest; in other cases, interference by society or the state with what people do can be argued for more easily, by reference to the interests of others individually, society collectively, or the state itself (and by appeal to the last avoiding the issue of paternalism completely).

Paternalistic action can be supported in several ways. A case can be made for it on utilitarian considerations, or argued in terms of justified belief about future vindication by its consequences and retrospective gratitude by its subject. There is a moral argument for paternalism, and also a pragmatic one. And lastly, a policy of paternalism may be based on ideological arguments, which assume a specific conception of a society and concomitant obligations entailed by the fact that a person belongs to it.

The Utilitarian Argument

Since I have said that I shall discuss only ostensibly self-regarding actions, utilitarian considerations present something of a paradox. A utilitarian argument in a social setting has to pay attention to its context, and this effectively rules out the possibility that any action is totally self-regarding, since the happiness of others as well as that of the agent must be taken account of in all felicific calculations. In strict terms it does not fall within my declared terms of reference which allow at least the conceivability of self-regarding actions. Nevertheless, the argument is worth mentioning with reference to what may be characterized as minimally other-regarding actions. People are social by nature, and each person—except for the rarest kind of hermit—is in some kind of relationship with others. Even the most self-regarding actions, therefore, take place physically within a community. It may be assumed that the agent who intends to affect others not at all by his actions is even so a member of a community, and thus it is possible for any action of his to be other-regarding.

Without taking account of the natural effects of a wrong or harmful self-regarding action on the agent's friends, relatives or associates through causing them, for example, sorrow or embarrassment, certain members of a community, particularly a close-knit one, are likely to feel anguish or sadness that one of their number, even otherwise a stranger to them, should act in a certain way. The proponent of a concept of a full autonomy in self-regarding actions would doubtless hold that though they might have such feelings, they have no right to give them any weight in their attitude towards the individual concerned. But does that individual have any right from a utilitarian position to ignore such feelings as misplaced or illegitimate? In fact, he does not, since utilitarianism has an empirical basis. An action, self-regarding though it may be for the agent, and from a common point entirely his or her own business, is all the same an action in a social context. As members of a community, people cannot disregard the indirect effects of their actions on others, even though they should believe those effects to be unwarranted. They must have regard for others even in their self-regarding actions; to view any action as *properly* only self-regarding, no matter what others think, is simply selfish. People should restrain themselves from acting in ways that may bring sadness to others; they should do so for utilitarian reasons: for example, the foregoing of a momentary pleasure or whim on their part will forestall the creation of possibly enduring sadness in others.

With regard to this first argument, discussion of a policy of censorship must predominantly be about the moral kind and relate to private immorality. By virtue of the concept of the political there can be no self-regarding actions for political censorship, and as far as religious thought is in question, we should perhaps see actions as other-regarding in a special way, since the individual is believed to be always in some relation to a supreme being. Even the mere presence, if known, of entirely private and solitary, but immoral, behaviour has a social setting and therefore may cause others offence. Although discreet, the widespread availability of material of an immoral kind may be a source of unease, hurt or outrage for many. To seek to root out immoral actions and suppress offensive publications, although no actual direct harm to others may be caused by them, can, as paternalistic interference, be adequately justified on utilitarian grounds.

The Consequentialist Argument

This argument need take into account only the interests of the individual himself. It is familiar enough: the person who acts interferingly towards another may genuinely believe that the latter, saved (let us say) from suicide or excessive drinking, or more positively, compulsorily educated along certain lines, will be happier and grateful in the future for the paternalistic benevolence shown him. Since he will be better off in the future for the present action—and will not only be better off but also subjectively feel himself so—this action can be held to be justified. The consequentialist will hold that the outcome vindicates both subjectively (for the individual concerned) and objectively (for society as a whole) the measures taken. Although critics may claim that this shows unpardonable presumption on the part of the paternalistic authority, this presumptive behaviour can be argued for on a rule-basis.

The individual may be retrospectively grateful for a change wrought in him without his consent. Like St Augustine we may pray that we be given chastity but not yet: nevertheless we recognize virtue for what it is, and once we come to possess it ourselves we look back on our past misdemeanours with regret that we ever committed them. If the virtue was 'forced' upon us we may still be grateful to our benefactor. Similar arguments are used in partial support of the imposition of unpopular economic and social measures: those unwillingly affected will be thankful for the good they were obliged to accept—or at least they will come to realize its rightness—at a later date. Similarly measures of censorship may be imposed to further moral, religious, political or social aims; it might be argued in their support that those who resent them at the time will see their wisdom and appreciate them on realizing the good that has been done both to society and to most of its members as individuals.

The Moral Argument

In the English-speaking world this argument seems to provoke the most fervent objections from the opponents of paternalism. It bases itself on the idea of an objective morality or of an established intersubjective or social morality. Those who would argue for interference on this basis must hold that certain actions are wrong *simpliciter* and must be prevented wherever possible, even when they are entirely self-regarding and cannot affect any other person. After all, some people may feel it to be wrong in terms of their own personal morality *not* to interfere with an individual acting foolishly, harmfully or sinfully towards himself. For them the omission or wilful failure to prevent such an action when they could attempt to do so may be morally equivalent to aiding or abetting that action.

Arguments about the problems of subjectivity and objectivity in morality and their consequences can hardly be discussed on the present occasion. If these problems are left to one side, what point relevant to the purposes of this study ought to be made about the moral argument? This argument rejects the claim that individuals are always the best judges of their own moral interests and, further, denies that they are morally autonomous, even in those self-regarding actions that are *solely* to their own detriment. In this respect the moral argument brings to the fore the essential social aspect of morality and makes it paramount. Anti-paternalists appear to be claiming that morality is essentially an individual phenomenon, whereas for their position on self-regarding actions to be justified they should rather assert that morality does not exist at all in any objectifiable way but is at best a subjective system of value-judgments peculiar to each individual. If morality is a social institution or has a social basis, paternalism and interference are justified: indeed they are an intergral part of moral behaviour.

The moral argument needs little comment in relation to the particular province of censorship. If it provides a justification for action at all, it will certainly justify censorship in association with the severe curtailment of many liberties, including freedom of expression and information.

The Pragmatic Argument

While any one self-regarding action may do no harm to others or to society as a whole, the collective or cumulative effect of many self-regarding actions may be damaging to other people and to the social structure itself. A number of suicides can be tolerated, from a practical point of view, in any society, but beyond a certain limit some sanction must be imposed or some kind of educational programme inaugurated in an effort to prevent an excessive number of people committing suicide; an excess of suicides, though each individually may be a wholly self-regarding action, could both disturb and alarm the surviving members of society, and if it did not do that, it would certainly dislocate the organization and stability of society. Likewise, an overwhelming preference for homosexual activity could threaten a society's continued existence and require measures to curb or repress it for that reason. Related to this point is the consideration that an excessive number of suicides or a general distaste for heterosexual relations would suggest that there was something amiss with society itself: there is surely some malfunction present in a society whose members are rejecting it or contributing to its demise. To attack the symptoms alone without understanding the causes is not to cure the sickness: to prevent suicides is not to rectify that possible social fault which is the cause of an excessive number of suicides. But might it not be felt that those in authority would be right in attempting to prevent suicides as far as possible by some direct method while the underlying social malaise was tackled and rectified in the longer term? One might go further and say that in the practical interests of society they would be justified in preventing suicides simply to avoid detrimental real effects for society, even though they might have no interest in attacking its fundamental causes.

This argument can be applied to censorship analogously with other interventionist measures. A certain amount of immoral activity, subversive ideas or antisocial expression may be seen as consisting simply of individual acts which, though hardly approved, are socially tolerable from the practical point of view insofar as they present no structural danger to society. Beyond a certain limit the number of individual acts may collectively come to present a real threat to society and, further, may be regarded as a sign that something is socially amiss. A flood of pornography may suggest that there is something wrong with a community's social psychology, just as a flood of subversive literature may be a sign that there is something at fault in its political structure. In addition it can be contended that, if allowed to continue freely, such manifestations tend to aggravate any social malaise by acting as a stimulus to further expression, and that in any case they cannot normally be regarded as desirable in themselves. To restrict such expression while the trouble itself is attacked and remedied may seem a reasonable policy in appropriate circumstances. And it is a policy naturally followed in other matters.

The Ideological Argument

Each suicide is in itself an individual act and may, for the sake of the present argument, be held to be an ostensibly self-regarding one also. But the need to rectify the collective phenomenon in the practical interests of others will lead to the realization that the number of suicides is a social phenomenon and may have its cause in the social structure. However insignificant in itself, the individual act, although seemingly self-contained, is not alone an *individual* act but still a *social* one. It is the result of social as well as psychological or even genetic influences and an act that takes place in society and has a social meaning. Even in their most private moments people cannot divest themselves of their social character.

The social or ideological argument incorporates elements of the previous two arguments discussed, namely the moral and the pragmatic. It includes the moral argument because paternalistic authority can only take acceptable action against an individual in the name of social morality. It includes the pragmatic argument because the social forces have practical effects, and it may be these which draw our attention to and justify ideological action. For practical purposes alone, each person is free to act so long as in making use of freedom he or she does not, individually or collectively with others, place the stability or the very existence of society in jeopardy. The curtailment of liberties in the interests of national security is an excellent illustration of the use of both pragmatic and ideological arguments to justify the primacy of society over the individual in relevant areas.

The ideological argument, however, is more than a combination of the pragmatic and moral arguments. Social attitudes, whether manifested in the majority of the population or in those who possess power or authority over it, depend finally not on pragmatic needs but on matters of principle. Thus a few individuals may engage in resistance against an enemy regime and carry with them, sympathetically, the majority of their fellow-citizens because they embody a social expression to which the others give their support. It is on a matter of social principle that members of a society resist when it is, for example, to their economic disadvantage as individuals to do so. The preservation or enhancement of society may be to the disadvantage of many of its individual members and even to the relatively long-term discomfiture of almost all of them considered as individuals. But it will be to the advantage of the society insofar as it has its continued existence ensured. In times of war or social stress, under the threat of famine, disease or other natural calamities, the individual may not simply be subordinated to society by social pressures or legal coercion, but may willingly subordinate himself in the interests not of other individuals so much as of society as a whole. With the ideological argument, therefore, paternalism ceases to be a concern primarily directed to individuals and becomes one centred on society itself.

The ideological argument places censorship along with other policies in the context of a society in which there is present one dominating ideology. If we may talk of the members of a homogeneous society possessing common ideals, similar aims, shared purposes, and agreement on many substantive matters, then policies involving restrictions on freedom of expression and the dissemination of ideas would seem natural social features. It is possible in some societies for such measures to be accepted by those persons against whom they are directed, in recognition of their citizenship and their obligation to respect the collectively expressed wishes of their fellow-citizens.

Paternalism and Free Speech

Paternalistic policies and other forms of interference by authority seem naturally to include measures of censorship. Superficially they are as applicable in the area of free speech as in other areas. If paternalism and interference with people's private actions are going to be allowed at all in their own or others' interests, there seems no reason that our freedom of expression too should not be curtailed on analogous lines. However, this is to beg the question whether areas like the expression of opinion and the dissemination of knowledge and ideas are not essentially dissimilar to the other areas in which tolerated and even welcome intervention occurs at the present time. People are no longer the final judges in many aspects of their own welfare, but perhaps there is yet some special reason for each person still to be the final judge in matters connected with his or her freedom of speech.

One way in which we might argue that free speech presents a special case even in an interventionist state is the following. As far as paternalistic or interfering measures in other fields are concerned, they are seeking to establish a social or economic equality, even in some cases going so far as to make use of 'positive discrimination' or 'affirmative action' to this end; through social equality will come a 'real' equality of rights to replace that so-called equality of rights which already exists for some people but is supposedly denied to many by reason of their social, economic or intellectual disabilities. Paternalism in effect denies equality now in order that a more perfect equality may be established in the future. A discussion of the rights and wrongs—or the realities—of such claims is hardly relevant here. What it is important to consider is that freedom of speech has little bearing on the social or economic equality that matters so much to us today. Its denial would not substantially further any egalitarian aims of this kind, whether social or economic. My freedom to spend my money as I like, on private hospital treatment, for example, or on the education of my children, results in actions which threaten the ideal of social equality. For the egalitarian, therefore, these actions are to be discouraged, and my corresponding freedom curtailed, if not entirely abrogated. Thereby the principle of equality is protected, even if the result of doing so is more to the disadvantage of some than the advantage of others. However, free speech, particularly in previously sensitive areas like morality, for the most part is neither here nor there as far as equality is concerned. (It should be noted that it may occasionally have a social significance. The expression of socially unacceptable ideas on racial matters can effectively be banned; and to speak out in the 'wrong' way on industrial relations, say, on the provision of social welfare benefits or on many other political concerns may be vehemently condemned as 'provocative' or 'socially divisive' or dismissed as 'unhelpful'. In short, with whatever adjective they are described, the opinions expressed are attacked emotively rather than criticized thoughtfully.) Free speech, therefore, comes to acquire the aura which originally surrounded the idea of liberty in general. Freedom of expression and information can still be preserved as an absolute individual right in what is otherwise an interventionist and restrictive society.

It can be seen, however, that when free speech is left alone in an interventionist society, it is not as a matter of principle with a bearing on the propriety of state interference in other areas. There is no principle of protection for free speech as such, as can be seen in connection with race relations, for in Great Britain it is no longer necessary for words to be intended to cause hatred but only that they should be likely to do so. If social conditions, and sometimes political conditions, justify interference, free speech will be interfered with. When it is left alone, one suspects that

that is for largely pragmatic reasons, principally because it threatens no substantial harm. Consideration of what may be called the practical criteria of interference does not suggest a special status for freedom of speech. Yet it seems possible that free speech may occupy a special position; it will be the purpose of subsequent sections to discuss how this is so.

The Adult's Claim to Free Speech

All responsible adults are to be treated as equal and autonomous insofar as their right to express themselves is concerned; this is the prevailing belief in a liberal democracy. No one (including the state) has the right to interfere other than on the grounds of the maintenance of public order against a more or less immediate threat. Restrictions are not to be imposed on grounds relating solely to the intellectual content of the knowledge or opinions expressed. The idea that 'public order', simply interpreted, is the only ground (except for one or two other special cases) for interference with freedom of speech will be treated below.[9] But wider grounds for interference do not necessarily conflict with the concept of equality. Although the imposition of censorship requires some kind of authority to examine material and impose restrictions, the structure of such authority need not be anti-egalitarian in principle. It could be constituted by a committee of delegates or elected representatives, and although such a structure must raise difficulties for a democratic theory which includes as one of its principles freedom of information, these difficulties are entailed by the task that has to be done—a task required in any state at least by the needs of national security—and as such must be regarded merely as anomalous rather than as a threat to basic principles.[10] It is not the way in which censorship is carried out that conflicts with a concept of equality, but rather the purposes for which it is employed.

State interference with what people do is not motivated only by the desire to protect others from the harmful or unwanted consequences of a person's actions. Rationality is defined in a way which excludes some kinds of self-regarding actions from its domain, it thereby allows society through law to categorize people as abnormal or of unsound mind, which in turn authorizes paternalistic intervention. I need only mention other well-known examples of behaviour that is not permitted even when entirely self-regarding, such as drug-taking, or exclusively confined to a consensual group, such as certain kinds of sexual acts, as well as moral concerns about homelessness and destitution which suggest that we do not automatically leave adults alone—unless they conform to certain approved, though admittedly loosely defined, models.

The argument for paternalistic treatment of children is that with children we are preparing them for a stage when they will be left alone to make up their own minds. The same argument cannot be adapted for adults. When the state treats adults in the same way, it is arrogating to itself the right to protect and guide them for an indefinite period into the future. With children we aim at the final goal of independence; we nurture them protectively as a preparation, through a proper development of their capabilities, for the day when they are due to take care of themselves, acting as fully independent adults. If we treat adults in the same way there can be no such goal.[11] In short, our paternalistic treatment of children is forward-looking, with its end found in a future stage of their lives, namely adulthood.

Whatever the niceties of such a view as part of the justification of some ethical theories, actual states of affairs belie it as a possible justification for measures taken in our own society and others like it. Compulsory measures are taken towards adults and obligatory restrictions imposed on them because they do not look after themselves in a socially endorsed manner, cannot be expected to do so, or be persuaded or educated into doing so. Paternalism is frequently a response to immediate problems but continues indefinitely, with no future goal in view which would allow the supersession or abandonment of necessary measures. Nevertheless, it may be the case that restriction of intellectual freedom has a different function in relation to children from its function in relation to adults.

In the United Kingdom, at the age of eighteen (as at similar ages in other countries) the normal child becomes completely an adult and receives all the adult's privileges and responsibilities, whatever they may be, no matter what success the 'preparation for life' has achieved. The terminal point for childhood restrictions has little or no connection in practice with actual preparedness for being an adult. It has been shown that the reason for a fixed age must be based on the concept of adult equality. However, a concept of adulthood could still exist without a fixed age for the attainment of adult status. It would be possible to prolong restrictions into physical maturity for some persons, but not necessarily for the rest of their lives. Even with adults there could still be a final goal of independence when the desired standard was achieved.

Paternalistic restrictive education of children has an apparent goal, namely an adequate preparation for life. Where other kinds of education or training have a goal there is some qualification or mark of success at the end of it. The qualification need not be a matter of strict assessment; it may be the attainment of a more or less informal status. If the relevant qualification is not gained, then a person must either continue with the educative process or give up trying to achieve his goal. This applies to many kinds of activities in similar ways, to the person who is a learner-driver or a plumber's apprentice, to the person who is learning to swim or trying to write a novel, to the undergraduate who is reading French for an honours degree as well as to the continental truck-driver who is picking up the French he needs in the course of his work. Each is working towards a level of achievement which can be marked by the award of a formal qualification, or more informally by the qualification of success, as when the aspiring novelist has his first book accepted for publication or the truck-driver is treated like a native-speaker and is able to respond accordingly. If a person goes through any kind of learning process and does not attain the required standard he is not generally regarded as competent in relevant matters. We attach importance to certain skills and look on the educative process as incomplete or unsuccessful if the skills have not been acquired.

With educational processes of all kinds there is some way of assessing competence and achievement. And we do make assessments. We do not consider someone *fully* competent to practise as an accountant just because he or she has attended relevant courses at a college. We do not regard a person as prepared for driving a car without supervision just because he or she has taken a set number of driving lessons. If the requisite standard has not been attained, then we should say that people must either go on learning, and continue to be treated as learners, or give up trying; and if the latter course is chosen, then it is also correct for us to say that where the activity is required of them—where the self-employed person needs an accountant, or where someone who cannot drive needs to get from one place to another by private car—that activity will have to be carried out for them by someone else or, in appropriate cases, someone else will tell them what they have to do and how they are to do it.

The fact that we take educative measures socially in some area of life has three implications. First, we regard this area as being important for people in society. Second, we believe that we have some kind of standard of assessment, and this connotes that it makes sense to talk of some reaching that standard and others not doing so, and of our being able to know whether they have. Third, a failure to reach that standard disqualifies (sometimes only in a *de facto* way) people from engaging in the activity at a specified level. This at least is our attitude to all educative measures except those which seem broadly to come under the description of preparation for adult life, but there seems no special reason why these preparatory measures could not be regarded in the same way.

The child is treated paternalistically with adult independence in view and with the goal of making the best use of that independence. Given the reasons for paternalistic education of children there seems no reason for not continuing restrictions as long as necessary for older people who do not appear to have attained the set standards. It is not, therefore, fruitful or apposite to make a distinction between children and adults in order to justify our paternalistic treatment of the former. Restrictions in children's education are both protective and formative, but their rationale is cut across by the notion of a *special* treatment of adults in the matter of freedom of expression and information.

Adults may or may not be 'prepared for life'; socially and politically, within wide limits, it is of no consequence. In many western societies there is an individualistic presupposition that adults should be free and independent, in thought completely, and in the expression of their opinions, in their access to information, and in their communications with each other about knowledge and ideas, as far as practical conditions permit. These individualistic ideas used also to extend to many other fields, especially to self-regarding actions. Nineteenth- and twentieth-century legislation has had the consequence that they have largely been abandoned, or are in the process of being abandoned, in many countries (and not least in the United Kingdom). Yet the special conception of the individual and autonomous adult entirely sovereign in the matter of personal opinion remains in the realm of free speech. Although interference with this freedom can be justified for one reason or another in society's treatment of children there can be no question of justification for the similar treatment of rational and responsible adults. That at least is the most generally accepted belief. I shall now go on to explore why this is so and how one might justify the special position of free speech in the life of an adult.

Free Speech as an Absolute Right

Are censorship and other restrictions on free speech peculiarly offensive because freedom of expression is a fundamental human right? An affirmative answer to this question might be justified by reference to the special place language has in human life. It is not trivial or facetious to say that people have the right to free speech because only human beings have the power of speech. With this power comes thought, and with thought comes the ability to think rationally and choose for oneself and for others. Language determines and delineates the full form of human life; a restriction of free expression is therefore tantamount to an attack on the very essence of being human. In short, to silence people is partially to deny their humanity and show disdain for the Kantian principle of 'respect for persons'.

An argument along such lines could be developed very persuasively, but it ought to be shown that if freedom of speech is truly an absolute human right, two premises require to be established, or at least assumed explicitly.

The first premise is the paramountcy of an absolute individualism. If freedom of speech is an absolute right, it is a right for all people; and it could be based not on any kind of moderate individualistic theory but only on an extreme individualism. It would not be necessary to claim that a person's freedom could never be limited, but any restriction would have to be with the full consent of the person concerned; and because free speech is an *absolute* right, that person could never sign away all of his or her freedom for good. Each person would always retain a right to disavow the restrictions and reclaim total freedom of speech. The right to free speech could not be taken away without express consent, and then only in a limited and temporary fashion.[12] In this situation the individual would be sovereign; neither the interests of society nor those of others could ever as a matter of principle overrule the freedom of all to express themselves individually in whatever ways they might choose. A society could be based on no more than a crudely simple contract theory, with each individual possessing an ever-present right to opt out of the contract at any time.

An absolute right to free speech would seem to present no insuperable obstacles to the continued existence of a rudimentary society, although nothing more sophisticated in the way of social organization could survive for very long. On the other hand, it could present great difficulties for a society which found itself under some kind of threat, for there would seem to be no possibility of reconciliation between an absolute right to free speech and the demands of national security. The interests of the security of the state and its citizens are not infrequently used to justify extreme or unnecessary restrictive measures; nevertheless, if there is going to be any place at all in a political scheme for national security, it has to be allowed that some restrictions on individual behaviour are justified and proper, and these include restrictions on the communication of information (naturally enough) and, in wartime, also on the expression of opinion.

However, I have suggested that restrictions in the interests of national security can be marked off from other areas of censorship. Given that a person's need to live securely in some kind of group necessitates the surrender of a measure of independence to other members of the group, the loss of an absolute right to freedom in the area of national security can be tolerated if it is assumed that a surrender of freedom in this area is going to be used by those acting on behalf of society in as sparing a way as possible. Restrictions in the name of national security can be accommodated under the minimal state principle along with other measures required to protect citizens against physical dangers.

Beyond this need to preserve the formal basis of their social lives, do people have a right to free speech in all other areas? The claim that they have an absolute right to it requires the most thoroughgoing individualism in every aspect of life, and it is questionable how viable a society might be, or indeed how much of a society it would be, if only the most elementary considerations were given to a physical or formal conception of national security.

The second premise necessary for free speech as an absolute right is a belief in the paramountcy of opinions, knowledge and ideas, and what may be called a general honesty of intellectual life. To justify a right to free speech by a claim that language, thought and reason are intrinsic characteristics of people which cannot be restricted without doing violence to the very concept of a person implies strongly that all the objects of censorship are truth-seeking arguments or high-minded expressions of reasoned opinion. This, of course, the objects of censorship frequently are not. Hard-core pornography, defamatory lies and fraudulent advertising are three indisputable examples which come immediately to mind of the frequent absence of high-mindedness in the use of the right to free speech. These abuses are also essentially human, it is true; one could perhaps argue for complete freedom in these and similar areas on the ground that they are as typically human as rational argument—and perhaps, cynics might say, more so. Nevertheless, no one would seriously want to argue that their suppression derogates from our humanity.

It is in regard to such manifestations of unrestricted free speech as pornography or defamation that freedom of expression as a principle encounters its limiting cases. These abuses mock free speech. The situation reminds us of the dilemma of toleration. The tolerant society or state, faced with people preaching intolerance with some (actual or possible) measure of success, must choose between tolerating the intolerant and thereby placing its own tolerant society in jeopardy, or refusing to tolerate them in order to protect the principle of toleration from those who would destroy it, but thereby becoming intolerant itself. (As an aside, what is the society with a belief in absolute freedom of speech to do about those of its members who may vociferously and persuasively advocate censorship?) To limit freedom of speech, however high-minded the motives may be for doing so, is, for that person who has the authority to set limits, to impose his or her own opinions, beliefs and values on others and diminish their personal autonomy, even if nothing worse is done and the truth is mistakenly destroyed.

For those who hold that free speech is an absolute right, intellectual honesty requires that all manner of expressions of opinion are tolerated in its name. Freedom of expression must be maintained, however worthless its particular realization may be. An absolutely free society must allow freedom to all kinds of expression, however unworthy they may seem or however much they may mock a well-intentioned principle of free speech, which exists in theory to give freedom to truth and reason. Absolute freedom of speech threatens serious values by refusing to distinguish reason from unreason or truth from falsehood. As I have suggested already, it cannot be presumed that truth and reason are bound to survive all manner of assaults because of their innate value.

Freedom of Expression and Freedom of Thought

The freedoms of expression and information have significance in themselves, but to confine discussion to them alone understates the problem of censorship and its extent. Censorship is related to freedom of thought itself, and claims that censorship leads *only* to restrictions on the expression, publication and dissemination of ideas cannot be totally accepted when we take account of, in the first place, 'commonsense' reasons about how freedom of expression and freedom of thought must be linked and, in the second place, deeper philosophical and sociological arguments, which are perhaps more open to debate, regarding the nature of thought itself.

It might be maintained that outside the Orwellian world of *Nineteen Eighty-four* freedom of thought, even with the sophisticated restrictive techniques of today, simply is not *necessarily* in question, and for the ordinary person is not in question even as a matter of practical possibility. Others cannot tamper with my freedom to think as I please. In normal circumstances there can be no direct attack on freedom of thought. Techniques of brainwashing have been used, but these require at present the concentration of resources on a small number of individuals and are unreliable in their effects; such techniques could not be used on the population as a whole or a sizable proportion of it. However, to think that freedom of thought was thereby guaranteed inviolability would be mistaken; thought is tied to expression in three clear ways.

First, my inability to acquire certain information, to be acquainted with certain opinions, or to have access to certain ideas cannot fail to have a profound effect on my own thinking. The possibility that we might develop our own ideas by our own unaided efforts is small indeed. Knowledge is a cumulative effort, to which each of us makes an individual contribution. Even the genius who takes an apparently solitary giant stride in some area of knowledge or brings about a revolutionary *bouleversement* of ideas in some field, does so within and because of the context of a body of solid knowledge which has been acquired by him, as one might say, ready-made. Even the brilliant theories of Galileo, Newton, Maxwell and Einstein, which each effected a radical change in the character of physical science, were built on the foundation of other people's work, and not so much on those people's failures as on their inability (whether through personal or social circumstances) to think through *completely* the implications of their own discoveries. My own freedom to think as I please is crucially dependent on my ability to have access to the thoughts of others; and therefore it further depends on the ability of others to express themselves freely and communicate successfully. If the state clamps down on general freedom of expression and information, it is indirectly, but none the less effectively, restricting not just the expression of thought but the process of thinking itself. Certainly, in connection with the prevention of subversion it may be suggested that one of the intentions of censorship, if not its direct aim, is the restriction of thought.

Second, if freedom of thought is dependent on the possession by others of freedom of expression, the proper and fertile development of my thinking will be very much bound up in a give-and-take with others: true freedom of thought requires for its proper continuation and development freedom of communication, which is also the freedom of exchange. What we are concerned with here is in part a freedom of *collective* thought. Ideas are not the creatures of one individual but the property of many, and for their full realization require the dissemination which promotes interaction. Insofar as it restricts (and is designed to restrict) freedom of communication through its restraints on expression censorship will once again impede the proper development of ideas and will therefore bring about effective restriction on freedom of thought.

Third, it is obvious that freedom of thought requires freedom of expression in the sense of the thinker's freedom to speak, so that others may have the benefits of communication with that person in their own work and the consequent development of their own thought. To attain their full value, freedom of information and communication naturally require freedom of expression. More deeply, what is individual freedom to think if people do not have the freedom to speak their thoughts? If people are obliged to confine their thoughts to themselves those thoughts are devalued, for people are social beings and their activities are given meaning by a social context. Thought possesses little value if it becomes a mere solipsistic activity. It may, correctly speaking, not be intrinsically without value, but it becomes pointless and, practically, of no real worth. The true value of people's thoughts is a social value.

To deny freedom of expression is to emasculate thought and leave it with a freedom that is empty and thus no real freedom at all. Denied the facility of expression we may justly claim that there is no freedom of thought. Much of the value that individual thinking has is created through the interrelations that people have with each other.[13] In practice, thought and expression must be considered together as the foci of a single freedom. Without freedom of expression all other freedoms may be lost, for, as I shall show, they are guaranteed by freedom of thought.

The links between thought and expression on which I have commented above are immediately obvious and relate to practical effects. There is a deeper, conceptual connection between the two freedoms, with effects which become more evident when censorship and other restrictions have been present in society for a considerable period of time. Then the effects of restrictions are no longer confined to the surface but have penetrated the structure itself. Readers may recall that one main intent of Newspeak in Orwell's *Nineteen Eighty-four* was to make heretical or subversive thought actually impossible. A potential rebel would simply not have the words available—and thereby be denied the concepts necessary—to take rebellious inclinations through to conscious development. Indeed, any attempts to do so would, if Newspeak was successful, turn out to be counterproductive: they would actually reinforce, conceptually, the would-be rebel's acceptance of the status quo. To limit our language is to limit our world.

No censor yet aspires to such accomplishments, but the results of successful and prolonged censorship, although smaller, are on the same lines. Words and concepts are not the self-made property of individuals; people do not derive the words they use from their own independent experience of the world. They are learned from society. Our experience of the world is mediated through concepts which our society has given us. The animal caged from birth has no notion of a free life; people who have grown up in a successfully restrictive society will be unaware that their personal freedom has been curtailed, because their language has come to define their world, and in turn that world determines their language. The ideal aim of restrictions should be to obliterate all memory or trace of a way of thinking so that at last no restrictions will be necessary. If we have not learned the concepts in question—if we cannot even learn of them—then we cannot think about the problems they raise. Language is public, and its concepts are public. Anything that entirely ceases to be public will be lost to language and thereby to thought. A complete loss of some way of thinking is not likely (although it is not impossible), but the weakening of conceptual power may be serious enough to distort and debilitate certain possibilities for thought.

Free Speech as a Guarantee of Other Freedoms

It is important to confirm the intimate link between freedom of expression and freedom of thought, because it supports the claim that freedom of expression occupies a special place apart from other freedoms. Elsewhere I have stated that these other freedoms lack the sacrosanct quality of freedom of speech. Many of them are directly connected with the possibility of action, and because of this contrast with freedom of thought and expression it will be adequate to refer to them all by the term 'freedoms of action'.

Freedom of speech and freedoms of action are on different levels. How is this so? The answer is simple. The abrogation of some particular freedom of action is reversible, whereas the abrogation of freedom of thought in part of the realm of ideas is not. Let us imagine that the freedom to travel outside one's own country is taken away: it is quite possible that later the ban is lifted or modified and the possibility of travelling freely is wholly or partially restored, perhaps as the result of reconsideration following representations to the government by those affected. Or again let us imagine that the economic freedom to adjust prices according to market forces is overruled by the state so that prices have to be fixed in a partly arbitrary and distorting manner. The processes of production and distribution go awry, but theoretical research, coupled perhaps with experimental procedures, instigated by economists or others with appropriate knowledge leads to the eventual re-establishment of a more sensible and efficient system. Or lastly, let us imagine that the freedom to choose the education of one's child is denied by the establishment of a single rigidly allocative system; it is possible that public demand and the arguments of educational theorists could successfully bring about the reintroduction of a system involving parental choice.

What is common to all these examples? Simply, it is that freedom of speech has brought about the restoration of some lost freedom of action. However, when thoughts themselves are effectively consigned to oblivion a possibly irrevocable act is committed. Such destruction, it is true, has often not been successful, but we ought not to assume that it never will succeed in eliminating the expression of a certain range of thinking and, with that, its memory and even its very possibility. For a thousand years the western church successfully extirpated almost all heresies for ever; so successfully did it do so, indeed, that in many cases, with what distorted and patchy knowledge remains to us today, we can hardly conceive how such ideas—whatever they might have been—could have aroused human passions.

Thought cannot always rescue itself when once the freedom to think has been lost, but it is able to rescue and recall other freedoms of action when opportunity arises and conditions for the exercise of those freedoms become more favourable. It is true that opinions may be independently rediscovered, and beliefs and theories reworked and re-elaborated from first principles; but such occurrences are often a matter of chance, and some ideas may be lost for ever. What matters for the importance of freedom of thought is our conscious and reasoned ability to preserve or recover freedom. Through the freedom of thought, which itself requires the freedom of expression, other freedoms are preserved even when they are themselves in abeyance.

Freedom of thought is required, therefore, to provide the capability of recalling lost freedom of action wherever this might seem appropriate or useful, as will often be the case. The freedom of thought is our guarantee of other freedoms, our security when we are obliged to surrender them. With its loss our other freedoms may be forfeited without the chance of recovery and, for all we know, will be. Therefore, whatever other freedoms are restricted or suppressed altogether, it seems that freedom of thought must be preserved in order to forestall serious losses to humankind.[14]

Free Speech and the Human Spirit

We can vindicate in another way the seemingly special position accorded to freedom of expression. Without prejudging the merits of any position concerning mind-body dualism, I think it is fair to say that our concept of a person gives primacy to the mind over the body and thus to mental processes over physical processes. If a person's body is functioning normally, or if it can be artificially helped to regain its normal functions in a self-sustaining way, the majority of us do not regard that person as literally dead, for 'dead' is, in ordinary parlance, a physical word. Nevertheless, if the brain shows incontrovertible signs of irreparable damage (and I say 'incontrovertible' here only for the sake of argument) we accept that he or she is as good as dead, personal life has come to an end and personality is no longer present. Furthermore, the experiences which gave that life meaning and value have also come to an end. Some people believe that, despite the increasingly complex and efficient technical possibilities for sustaining life in the most adverse circumstances, it is morally acceptable, and even morally *right*, to discontinue life-supporting processes when life has permanently become nothing more than a physiological function. Indeed, some people would go further and argue that in appropriate circumstances it is a moral imperative to act positively and deliberately bring physical life to an end. On the other hand, when the brain is functioning normally or nearly so, although the body may be shattered, we believe that personality continues to exist. In consequence, it is right to do everything possible to preserve life unless account must be taken of special countervailing conditions such as the unrelievable suffering of unbearable pain. In short, there is a much greater presumption in favour of preserving life when it is the mental side rather than the physical side which continues to function.

This primacy which we accord to a person's mental existence is manifested also in general feelings about the proper character of punishment. Punishment by imprisonment, for example, is intended to incarcerate the body not the mind: the prisoner is encouraged to engage in educational study or worthwhile practical activities. Solitary confinement is believed to be wrong if it leads to serious mental distress in the prisoner. In more extreme cases physical torture is viewed with horror but mental torture is often held to be still worse. Given that we have, or could probably develop, psychochemical techniques for the reform of personality, it nevertheless seems part of the general consensus that to imprison a man for ten or twenty years (without successful reform in many cases) is ethically preferable to effecting his reform or cure over a period of a few weeks or months through pharmacological reconditioning or, more extremely, through brain surgery of a few hours' duration or other physical surgery, such as castration, even though he might then be safely given his freedom.

Such an attitude would seem neither to result from a leaning towards a retributivist theory of punishment and the belief that a person deserves to suffer for what he has done nor from an illusion about the efficacy of a long prison sentence as a deterrent, since one expects that potential lawbreakers would be as likely to be deterred by the prospect of a compulsory change of personality as by imprisonment. Many reform theorists are prepared to accept imprisonment pure and simple as a last resort rather than have recourse to 'unnatural' techniques of reform, for these are beyond the pale of consideration. Even to cure highly disapproved behaviour—for example, sexual perversion—by 'unnatural' methods is felt somehow not to be right, even though the subject might freely consent to such treatment and in some cases actually desire it. Attitudes to education show a corresponding similarity: teaching is to be sharply distinguished from indoctrination both by ordinary people and by some educationalists. The claim that there is a conceptual distinction is important in itself, even though there may be no sharp distinction in practice when educational processes are analysed. At a deeper level, both psychologically and philosophically, it is probably true to say that the two processes form a real as well as a conceptual continuum and in many cases could not be easily delineated from each other.

The common attitude which I have tried to illustrate here might be characterized as a dislike—or rather, abhorrence—of 'interference' with a person's mind. This ready antipathy could help to explain our differing attitudes to restrictions on various freedoms. Most restrictions on our freedoms—what I have generally referred to as freedoms of action—involve merely physical constraints or interference of a material kind (for example, financial disincentives). To restrict freedom of expression, on the other hand, is to attempt to constrain, change or suppress *thought*. To try to affect people's thoughts is an attempt to interfere with their minds. Denial of free speech, as a restriction of freedom of thought, touches the very core of a person's being in a way in which restrictions on a freedom of action, no matter how severe they may be, do not. In a central way they bear on a characteristic which is believed to mark out people as specifically human; this is their possession of rationality.

Free Speech and Rationality

On what philosophical principle might the idea of an absolute right to free speech be based? Mill's argument for liberty in general sets us at first in an apparently profitable direction.

> The reason for not interfering, unless for the sake of others, with a person's voluntary acts is consideration for his liberty. His voluntary choice is evidence that what he so chooses is desirable, or at least endurable, to him, and his good is on the whole best provided for by allowing him to take his own means of pursuing it.[15]

Mill includes the rider 'unless for the sake of others' here, but in his interpretation this applies only to the protection of the physical safety and material well-being of other adults and to the general safeguarding of children. Apart from these unexceptionable considerations the right to free speech should come under no restriction, for the expression of opinions directed towards adults ordinarily presents them with no immediate physical threat, and society has no right to prevent their access to any kind of information, opinion or entertainment which they might desire. Mill's conception of the right to freedom of expression was as absolute as such a concept may ever be.

What is the foundation for Mill's assertion of this freedom? The answer is simple and well known: people who are unhampered in exercising their own free will are bound to make their choices thoughtfully and in their own good interests. It is generally agreed that Mill's concept of the typical adult was over-rational; but if we could find some concept of rationality that was more reasonable, we might well be able to justify free speech as an absolute right along similar lines.

The nineteenth-century liberal held to a general principle of freedom in almost all areas of life; today the sort of freedom envisaged has to all intents and purposes been lost, abrogated or substantially impaired. This has been the result as much of welfare policies to assist those in material need as of programmes to realize egalitarianism (and many social policies provide evidence of both characteristics). Both of these are themselves products of the liberal's programme. The consequence is that the freedom of expression which used to be one freedom among others (or, perhaps, first among equals) has been left to occupy a special position for us a century or more later. As mentioned earlier, restrictions on freedom of expression seem peculiarly offensive, especially in intellectual life. This freedom has become conceptually almost totally separated from other freedoms, although in the nineteenth century all freedoms, broadly speaking, had the same basis. For the Victorian liberal, the individual was to be freed from interference by the state, but this meant that he also had to look after himself. Whereas today, as Gertrude Himmelfarb has pointed out:

> The same liberals who insist upon the largest measure of individual liberty in one area—the freedom to see, read, say, and act as they please, to be free of moral constraints and social conventions—also tend to insist upon the largest measure of social and government controls in other areas—to provide for economic security, racial equality, social justice, environmental protection, and the like.[16]

This separation of freedom of expression from other freedoms seems capable of justification in terms of the idea of rationality. I shall argue first that other freedoms do not necessarily involve a concept of rationality, and then I shall discuss the nature of the concept of rationality required for the right to free speech, and the way in which it may appear to raise this freedom to a privileged position.

Rationality is not in question in those areas where freedom of a more or less material kind is concerned and in other areas of typically socialist intervention and state provision. If it were, it would be possible to argue from one or more of these cases to the case of free speech. If people are directed or persuaded (in a strong way) for their own good in matters of their material interest and in some areas of their intellectual welfare, why should it not be permissible for them to be constantly supervised for their own good in *all* spiritual and intellectual matters? For example, it would be possible for state support of the arts or state sponsorship of cultural and educational programmes and activities to progress from being a useful provision of financial resources for individuals and groups not typically overaffluent (and a consequent enhancement of their freedom) to becoming the means for discrimination, by way of financial pressures, against unsupported activities, publications and programmes. Naturally, the justification for this discrimination would be that it was for the public good.[17]

Rationality and Intervention

I intend to show that the arguments used in support of measures of largely material welfare cannot be validly extended to most measures of intellectual or spiritual welfare (with the notable exception of the education of children). Most interventionist measures by the state do not really have anything to do with a principle of rationality, even though we might at first think that freedoms are restricted or modified because they might be abused or even just not used in the best and most properly rational way. This claim is best substantiated by taking three different examples of kinds of state intervention which might be thought unfavourable to it. In addition, I shall give an example of a situation where rationality *is* involved but which is clearly a special case and, beyond other similar exceptional cases, does not possess a general application to many kinds of intervention.

The first example to be noted is the policy of compulsory education which prevails in all developed and most developing countries of the world.[18] Why is there such a policy? The universal provision of some basic type of education says nothing about rationality; or rather, it allows rational desires for the education of children to be realized when they might be thwarted for poor families, for example, by the expense of schooling. *Compulsory* education, however, ensures that even parents who do not want to send their children to school are obliged to do so, and that all children receive a broadly similar kind of education relating to some collectively held idea of basic requirements for life in society. The *prima facie* presumption would be that the education of a child is a rational desire and that the state steps in to enforce correct, rational action on the parents' part when this desire is absent. The presumption would be incorrect, for rationality as such dictates no particular kind of action here.[19] In this case the state steps in to enforce certain minimal *social* norms; it enforces only *one* kind of rational choice. One might argue a reasoned case that certain children should not be educated at all, or that children should be compulsorily educated to what is currently further- or higher-education level—a level which is fast becoming the *de facto* norm in many Western countries; and one could rationally argue against the making of what is much the same type of education obligatory for all children as well as against the setting of a rigidly fixed school-leaving age which pays no regard to the individual case. Compulsory education, in short, is a social policy; it has a rational basis insofar as it is believed to be the best means to some chosen social ends, but it has nothing to do with the rationality, or lack of it, of individual behaviour. This positive conception of an educational measure as embodying a social policy with aims beyond its immediate apparent intentions may be applied in like ways to measures of health and social welfare as well as to some economic policies.

A second example of state intervention is the increasing legal protection offered to people against fraudulent claims in advertising, the 'small print' in contracts, hidden obligations or the lack of a guarantee with some article or service they have bought. Surely, we should argue, the rational person would behave circumspectly, taking care to avoid suspicious bargains, questionable deals, badly drawn-up contracts, and other potential pitfalls. Does the protection offered by the state, then, presume lack of rationality? It does not; it would seem, rather, that these protective measures are taken on the presumption not of a lack of rationality on the ordinary person's part but of a lack of relevant knowledge or appropriate skill. The exercise of reason could well lead to the development of these skills; but in any person such development requires not simply reason but also the right sort of aptitude, intelligence, knowledge, and probably a large amount either of free time to investigate potential problems or of money to pay professionals to do so. Protective measures of this kind are taken to safeguard people from complexities which the ordinary person—even the ideally rational person—could not on the whole be expected to handle with a sufficient degree of competence.

A third example of paternalistic intervention is the way in which the state enforces through law the wearing of crash-helmets by motor-cyclists or of seat-belts by car drivers and passengers. Although there are innumerable safety measures to be applied in the workplace and elsewhere, this example is particularly important because it concerns purely private actions. Here, it seems is a measure directed unequivocally towards the prevention of behaviour that cannot be considered rational. Such measures surely presume, if any do, that many persons left to themselves will not behave in a rational way, for the only rational course of action when travelling is to make use of any safety equipment available; to fail to do so is to behave in a manner that is not rational. Yet again, I suggest, rationality is not in question here: the risk to the unprotected individual, for that individual alone, is statistically so small that to take that risk cannot straightforwardly be condemned as non-rational behaviour. After all, it is thought quite rational to take part in hazardous activities such as mountaineering or motor-racing or many more mundane sports, where the risks to life and limb are greater. The use of a crash-helmet or a seat-belt is the *most* rational way to behave; but rationality is not of a nature such that if one action is rational, alternative actions cannot be; the action that is less rational is not always less than rational. Not to take the most perfectly rational action in any circumstances is not thereby to fail to be rational at all. Rationality and irrationality admit of degree; some personal risks can be small enough to be rationally acceptable. In imposing certain legislative measures the state is, perhaps, taking steps to ensure that the most completely rational action in the circumstances is enforced, but it does not in doing so presume that those towards whom such measures are directed would otherwise behave in a non-rational or irrational way.[20]

I have suggested that there are exceptions to this claim that paternalistic intervention is not connected with rationality. The basis of state-control of the consumption of alcohol seems to be linked to consideration of rational behaviour. The state interferes with people in the interests, if not of preserving rationality, at least of keeping less than rational behaviour within certain limits. A rational decision to start drinking can lead indirectly but quickly to irrational behaviour; although temperate and moderate drinking does not affect the continuance of rational thought and action, the abuse of drink undoubtedly does. Through overindulgence in alcohol a person ceases to be rational; intoxication carries him or her straightforwardly into irrationality. And although legislation is not directed ostensibly just towards the maintenance of rationality, it is directed towards control of the causes and the manifest consequences of loss of rationality. A person can be responsible for starting with drink or drugs, but is not responsible (in a practical sense), and cannot be, for what he or she does while under the influence of them. Even the most supremely rational person would be unlikely to continue making rational decisions while under the influence of some drugs which have been taken voluntarily. Therefore, while people are in an intoxicated state, or when they place themselves in positions where it is possible that they will be, they forfeit their claim to be treated completely as rational, autonomous beings. Since they risk losing their rationality and therewith their capacity to be responsible for themselves, it is acceptable that the state should assume responsibility and enact measures controlling access to drink, providing for the detention, where appropriate, of those in a drunken state, and in some cases mandating or facilitating treatment.[21]

Paternalistic interference by the state, then, can be dismissed either as not generally being concerned with rational behaviour at all, insofar as no claim is made that the people affected are incapable of behaving rationally about the matters in question, or exceptionally as being linked to rationality in special cases where interference is directed against irrationality and its consequences. As far as the main body of cases is concerned, state interference can be completely reconciled with the continuing treatment of individuals as rational persons. If paternalistic legislation really presumed that many people were less than rational or that their capacity for rational thought and action needed supplementation in some way, the actual functioning of this legislation would conceivably be quite different. As it is, welfare benefits are provided, but there is a presumption that people will behave rationally and choose to claim them on their own initiative. If a person is caught breaking the seat-belt law, he or she will be answerable in court: legal responsibility assumes a capacity for rational thought and action.[22] Where the state acts paternalistically and without the presumption of full rationality, treatment of the individual concerned is very different. Thus the state treats children paternalistically, but not as possessing a full rational maturity. They are not treated as entirely responsible in law; for example, parents are responsible for their children's attendance at school up to a certain age, even though in many cases truancy is completely the child's action. The mentally subnormal or disturbed are treated paternalistically but not as rational persons: protection and welfare are given to some of them without their asking for such assistance and, from time to time, even against their wishes.

The Assumption of Rationality

Many state policies today are intended to affect people for their own good but involve a considerable loss of freedom. An individual's loss of immediate personal freedom for this reason has little connection in most cases with his or her treatment as a rational person. I have emphasized the irrelevance of irrationality in many areas where freedom is involved so that the bifurcation of liberal attitudes to freedom may be theoretically justified, not so much to account for the loss of freedom in areas other than freedom of speech, which can be done in many convincing ways, but rather to attempt to explain why free speech is still sacrosanct today and to provide a plausible basis for the conception of freedom of speech as an absolute right. Mill's argument for all freedoms rests on the idea of rationality; this is generally acknowledged. Indeed, his sanguine conception of the ordinary person's rationality is a frequent ground of criticism. However. the argument for free speech continues to depend on rationality, and it is this dependence that marks it off from other freedoms. What is required is a concept of rationality that will survive criticism and still be typical of ordinary people. The denial of people's freedom to express themselves or to have access to information has a special character different from restrictions on other freedoms. We do not treat people as rational when, through censorship, we restrict them in ways which attempt to channel their thoughts along desired lines. The loss of freedom of speech cannot provide direct parallels with the loss of freedom in such areas as education, welfare or personal safety, where our freedom, in a simple sense, is today much curtailed.

In the realm of national security restrictions on free speech have practical justifications, and one or two other areas (libel and slander, for example) can be accounted for in special ways. Outside these areas, and especially in seeking to impose standards where there is no question of a real threat to public order, or to implement policies intended to govern freedom of expression and information (and therefore, indirectly, freedom of thought itself), the state asserts a certain rationality in its proposed norms. It is saying that to think otherwise, or choose otherwise, is not what a rational person does. To censor serious political, religious or moral thought is to imply that it cannot be the choice of a rational person. By doing so, the state or other authority therefore treats adults as less than rational. How this is so I shall show in some detail.

It is part of a common notion of society that, where there is no direct evidence to the contrary in a particular case, its members should be treated as responsible individuals. Their being treated as responsible involves their being treated as rational. The idea that adults are, unless proved otherwise, rational persons is at the very heart of our political, social and economic structure. Representative democracy rests on a universal franchise which surely presupposes that electors are rational. Here we are not concerned with the *ideally* rational person (any more than we are with the ideally intelligent or ideally knowledgeable person), who would not require the paternalistic measures against which classical liberalism argues, but with the ordinary human being, who, after all, is a 'rational animal'. There is a kind of minimum freedom required for a person still to count as rational. There is an area from which state action must generally be excluded in order that the state's treatment of someone shall still accord with that person's status as a rational being.

For a person still to count as rational, a reasonable freedom of expression is necessary, covering ideas about political, moral and religious matters.[23] It is a commonplace that even well-educated, knowledgeable and cultured people frequently disagree about these. At the present time there are no acceptably proven claims that positions in morals, politics or religion are true or false, correct or incorrect. There is no rational way of showing once and for all which is the right view to adopt. This conclusion would seem to argue that if the state enforces morality of one particular kind, rationality need not enter at all into its justification for doing so. However, this is not so: there can be only two ways of justifying state actions in such an area. One way is by arguing for the practical necessity or expediency of the actions, as is exemplified by considerations of national security or physical public order. Although it is possible for the state to enjoin certain moral actions on practical grounds, if it does so they must cease to be *moral* actions in the state's eyes. To compel performance of a moral duty for practical reasons means that its morality has no relevant justifying force. If its justification is entirely in terms of practicality then the state is paying no attention to the moral quality of an action, and we may accordingly say that morality as such is of no consequence.

The only other justification of state action in the area of morality must be based on morality itself, that is, on a particular system of morality, involving 'legal moralism'.[24] The idea is a respectable one. Lord Devlin asserted that 'the criminal law as we know it is based upon moral principle', and that in some cases 'its function is simply to enforce a moral principle and nothing else';[25] it may be that many people are sympathetic to this point of view when fundamental moral values are at stake. Through the law the state makes claims about what is right and what is wrong. In doing so it claims not only that there can be such judgments but also that it makes these judgments rightly—in an absolute sense. It is necessary for it to make this *strong* claim: if it merely acted because *some* system of morality (but no particular one) was necessary for social cohesion, what it imposed would, firstly, lack ultimate moral conviction (which would come to nullify the basis of its claim) and, secondly, cease to be moral, since its justification would have reverted to pragmatism.[26] In implicitly denying relativism and asserting that its judgments are right, therefore, the state implies too that conflicting moral judgments are wrong. A claim about absolute moral rightness is a claim about moral truth and places such truth on a par with truth in other areas of human experience. Assertions of truth are properly founded on rational judgment, and what is absolutely right must therefore be what is rational. Morality can no longer be a matter for rational disagreement, any more than basic arithmetic can be. The evidence for moral judgments is open to all; if people persist in upholding conflicting judgments in the face of this evidence and society's position, they place their reason in question. Though this argument has been related here to moral questions, parallel arguments would hold in corresponding ways in matters of politics and religion. Stated abstractly, these points seem somewhat fanciful, and yet the self-evident rightness of democracy in our own political culture is a standing example of a value that most people are convinced is beyond question.

In imposing on people *moral* standards which are not their own, legal moralism, it seems, denies their rationality. But this does not show that by allowing freedom of expression the state agrees that all persons enjoying that freedom are rational. Is it not possible to hold that the existence of freedom of expression should suggest no conclusions at all about rationality? In fact, it is not, since even the most liberal state recognizes, as we all do, standards of rationality—or, rather, irrationality—in moral, political and religious behaviour and in free speech in general. While we recognize the possibility and the rightness of very extensive disagreement about moral standards we also recognize that moral behaviour of certain kinds just cannot be permitted—on moral grounds. Examples do not require elaboration. What is important is that there is general agreement that certain extreme behaviour is immoral and rationally unacceptable. In many cases there is full agreement about what is *not* rational. To repeat a familiar example: we cannot allow a man needlessly to shout 'Fire!' in a crowded theatre, not on account of inconvenience alone—sometimes freedom, like justice, must be asserted whatever the consequences—but also because this act can universally be deemed irrational because of its antisocial and dangerous nature. We do not have to imagine so potentially calamitous an act: we properly eject from a theatre a person who repeatedly interrupts the performance needlessly. (Whether we justifiably do so when the interruptions have a serious point is another matter.) There is the possibility that a distinction, however rudimentary, between the rational and the irrational may be drawn in areas where free speech is most important. People left alone to exercise their freedom are therefore being treated *prima facie* as rational.

In permitting a climate of free speech, of freedom in the publication and dissemination of ideas and in access to information, the state is implicitly treating the vast majority of its citizens as rational persons.

Reasonable free speech is a necessary concomitant of rationality, it appears; if people truly are rational animals, intellectual freedom of whatever kind cannot be denied them. Here we must be careful not to exaggerate the idea of a rational person so that it relates exclusively to the notion of someone who is ideally rational. Freedom of expression requires and presupposes not an ideal but simply a proper rationality—the sort of rationality which our treatment of adults as responsible leads us to expect of them. To deny such freedom may indeed be to imply that they are not truly people who should command our respect.

If freedom of speech is bound up with rationality in a way in which other freedoms are not, then it is a freedom of a special kind, and the arguments, perhaps involving social aims, used in support of measures that limit freedoms of a mostly material kind, cannot be extended without change to justify measures which lead to serious curtailment of freedom of expression and information. Arguments in favour of extensive free speech do not support arguments against the freedom of *laissez-faire* individualism in other areas of life; but the two positions are, in their relation to the idea of rationality at least, fully compatible. It remains to be seen whether considerations of rationality should bring debate about the individual's right to free speech to a conclusion.

Censorship and Privacy

One final concern still remains for consideration in this chapter. Although censorship is ostensibly concerned with public expression it impinges on people's private worlds. An important argument against certain areas in which censorship is enforced, rather than against censorship as such, relies on making a distinction between the public and the private. The realm of legal restrictions and prohibitions is thought to be properly confined to public speech. Any communication of ideas which occurs in private should consequently be free from the intervention of the law. But in the end can a distinction between 'publications' (in a literal, etymological sense) and other forms of expression be maintained?

In the present context there are two ways in which private acts tend to invalidate a claim based on the sanctity of privacy. First, they cease to be strictly private and may require restriction because what people say and how they act on what they say can acquire a certain publicity (and even, perhaps, a notoriety) by repute. Second, communication, however private, gives other people ideas, and while the process of private dissemination of an idea may be very slow, the result may be no different in kind from the result of its open publication.

First, private behaviour may become public by repute. Immoral actions, however apparently private or nominally concealed, through repute, gossip or hearsay become actions that are 'as good as' public. And if no action to counter publicity is taken, this is to the scandal of the morals of society. And if the situation continues unchecked, the 'private' actions may be as potentially subversive as the corresponding 'public' actions against which measures may habitually be taken. In such a case normal restrictive measures, it seems, may justifiably be applied to the private actions, including the expression of ideas.

To this it may be rejoined that the law should seek to be fair in making use of criteria regarding the publicity or privacy of actions. Specifically, there must figure here a consideration of the intentions of the individuals involved. Those who publish intentionally or negligently certain ideas or engage in certain kinds of behaviour which they know or should know to be unacceptable in the society in which they live are rightly to be punished (if the law under which they are punished is itself justified). But if their intention is to confine their speech or actions entirely within a private circle, and if they take all reasonable measures to ensure such privacy, should they not then be permitted complete freedom of expression or behaviour (with due account taken of other factors such as consent) within those limits?

To this the reply must be that the breaking down of privacy through gossip or notoriety rather than through intention or negligence cannot be considered an excusing factor. If society is concerned about the expression of ideas and the content of ideas expressed, if censorship is a consistent policy and is justified within the society, then the dissemination of ideas, however unintended, must be treated as a matter of absolute liability. Society directs—or should direct—its attention to the ideas expressed more than to the individuals responsible for expressing them. If a society is going to censor, the rationale of doing so is to prevent the dissemination of those ideas which are considered pernicious. It cannot in such cases begin to consider how such dissemination came about. If it becomes a stated policy aim of government to prevent the dissemination of harmful knowledge or opinion then the attempt must be made to achieve this aim, however such knowledge or acquaintance might have come about and by whatever measures necessary. If society is seeking to eliminate harmful opinions it is of no moment to consider the intentions of those who are the source of those opinions. To consider intentions can prove to be the beginning of profound weaknesses in both the purpose and the practice of censorship and of considerable confusion about it. For example, it is not clear why an artistic or scientific intent should render a work immune to censorship, since there is no reason to believe that its corrupting effect, if there is one, will be moderated on account of its presence.

The second way in which private acts may cease to be rightly considered as private is because of an examination of the possible results of what are (considered individually) private communications of ideas. A man or woman sitting at home with two or three friends may communicate privately to them personal knowledge or opinion. Those friends may the following day discuss the same ideas with other friends of their own, again quite privately; and these in turn may talk the ideas over privately with people they know. The result may be that in a matter of a few days the ideas concerned may have acquired wide currency and be as widespread as if they had been expressed openly at some public meeting. (And who knows what ideas may have arisen at first in this manner?) Obviously, there is still a real distinction to be made between 'public' and 'private', but is it one to be drawn here? Can there be a significance for the limits to free speech in a distinction between public expression and private communication? Since the preoccupation of censorship must be with undesired consequences, it seems clear that there cannot be.

The justification of restrictions on free speech is based on the content of ideas and opinions, their currency and their possible effects on individuals and society as a whole. The manner of their communication is therefore of no significance in principle, although in practice it may bear on what response, if any, a public authority deems necessary. That an objectionable idea, opinion or belief is not published generally and in public but is communicated slowly from one person to another is not germane to the issue of whether it is as a matter of fact entering the public domain and having a social effect. Restriction is justifiably related to practical consequences.

Notes

1 Mill, *op. cit.*, pp. 149–150.

2 Sir James Fitzjames Stephen, *Liberty, Equality, Fraternity* (Cambridge, 1967), p. 142.

3 *Ibid.*, p. 157.

4 *Cf.* Robert Downie and Elizabeth Telfer, *Respect for Persons* (London, 1969), p. 60.

5 This possibility was still present in 1960: see Mervyn Griffith-Jones's opening speech for the prosecution in the *Lady Chatterley's Lover* case, reprinted in *The Lady Chatterley's Lover Trial*, with an introduction by H. Montgomery Hyde (London, 1990), pp. 61–62.

6 For example, financial resources and networks of friends or relatives.

7 Bernard Williams, 'The idea of equality', in *Philosophy, Politics and Society (Second Series)*, edited by Peter Laslett and W.G. Runciman (Oxford, 1962), p. 116.

8 Mill, *op. cit.*, pp. 142–143.

9 See below, chapter 4.

10 Any theory of a free and open democracy inevitably stumbles over not only aspects of defence policy but also deliberations on monetary and economic affairs.

11 One favoured way of explaining the distinction between restrictions on a child and those on an adult is to argue that the former are designed so that the individual 'can eventually take over', whereas with the latter we are 'managing his life for him'. This distinction also justifies the different treatment of children and childlike adults. (*Cf.* Downie and Telfer, *op. cit.*, pp. 59–60.)

12 There is a parallel here with Mill's argument that people do not have the freedom, by their own deliberate choices, to sell themselves into slavery. See Mill, *op. cit.*, p. 173.

13 *Cf.* L.T. Hobhouse, *Liberalism* (London, 1911), pp. 27–28: 'Liberty of thought is of very little avail without liberty to exchange thoughts—since thought is mainly a social product; and so with liberty of thought goes [*sic*] liberty of speech and liberty of writing, printing and peaceable discussion.'

14 This point suggests a parallel with the distinction between principle and practice in censorship. See above, chapter 2.

15 Mill, *op. cit.*, p. 173.

16 *On Liberty and Liberalism* (New York, 1974), p. 324.

17 A current example of the consequences of too great a dependence on state support by supposedly independent institutions is the plight of British universities, which find their fundamental character not only disrupted by cuts in public spending but, more sinisterly, have their academic independence undermined as their work becomes increasingly subject to the directions of public policy and demands for greater 'efficiency'.

18 It could be argued that the state steps in to assert the rights of one individual, the child, against others, the parents, who might otherwise not see that it was properly educated; but the education of a child in Victorian times concerned the rights of one person only, namely the father. At the present time there may be a case for reasserting the rights of parents to make major decisions about the nature of their children's education.

19 *Cf.* Hume's well-known arguments that 'reason alone can never be a motive to any action of the will' and that 'it can never oppose passion in the direction of the will'. See David Hume, *A Treatise of Human Nature* (Oxford, 1888), p. 413.

20 Although not irrational for an individual not to take action, it might be irrational (or not rational) for the state not to do so, because, while the individual risk may be minimal, the totality of casualties and their social consequences can well be rationally unacceptable.

21 Mill rejects the idea of state interference with solitary drunkenness; yet we might see the argument in favour of interference as analogous to Mill's argument that there is no right to sell oneself into slavery. In doing the latter a man 'abdicates his liberty', which is not itself freedom; similarly, by indulging to excess in drink, he abdicates his rationality. (*Cf.* Mill, *op. cit.*, pp. 172–173.)

22 Responsibility remains in drunkenness but the person's drunken state is often taken into account as some kind of mitigating factor.

23 The liberal conception of a reasonable free speech is discussed by H.J. McCloskey, 'Liberty of conscience: its scope and limits', *Inquiry*, 13 (1970), pp. 219–237.

24 *Cf.* H.L.A. Hart: *Law, Liberty and Morality* (London, 1963), p. 6. He distinguished legal moralism from paternalism.

25 Devlin, *op. cit.*, p. 7.

26 Compare what Devlin had to say about the necessity of a common morality and its significance for society (*op. cit.*, pp. 12 ff.) with James Stephen's thoughts about the possibility of *truth* in religion and the foundation this provides for enforced morality (*op. cit.*, pp. 87 ff.).

4 Social Order

The Necessary Limits to Free Speech

John Locke is often considered to be one of the fathers of the liberal state; yet he refused toleration to those who threatened not merely the preservation of civil society as such but rather the essential character of the English society which existed at the time he was writing his political works. No kind of behaviour which might be accounted subversive, however peaceful outwardly, was to be tolerated.[1]

Subversion is often not included among the grounds of permissible restrictions on free speech in a liberal society. A neat formulation of a common liberal principle is: 'Liberty of expression should be left unrestricted except for the sake of protecting liberty, ensuring fair trials and legal hearings, preventing libel, defamation, fraud, or incitement to riotous behaviour.'[2]

Stated thus, the principle is both wider and narrower than Locke's principle of largely religious liberty; it is wider insofar as it covers matters not directly related to public order, such as libel and defamation, and narrower because it does not cover an important political phenomenon which Locke does, namely subversion. A theory of that minimal censorship which is all that liberals are in principle prepared to accept, requires examination in three areas: one area concerns central matters of public order, the second area covers subversion, which appears connected with order, albeit in an indirect way, while the third brings together issues associated with miscellaneous matters such as defamation, fraud and *sub judice* rules, which are not directly connected with public order but which rightly seem to require control in any society.

Defamation

Libel and slander are areas where free speech is properly limited; censorship, under whatever name, passes the test of validity, for who can take exception? The aim of anti-defamation laws is to inhibit defamatory speech. But for what reason? Defamation apparently has little or nothing to do in principle with public order; as a rule, it gives offence to an individual or a group but it is not a threat to society.

In including defamation along with other actions or activities to be prevented in any liberal state, few writers call attention to a distinguishing feature of legal actions for defamation: this is that libel cases reach the courts as the result of private civil actions between individuals as plaintiff and defendant. This special feature suggests that laws against defamation may not contribute to an understanding of the general principle which underlies minimal restrictions on free speech. Nevertheless, the existence of state-backed legal provisions which include publicly enforced sanctions creates a strong tendency for libel to be avoided by self-restraint. It could be argued that this preventive effect makes libel law no different in practice from most other kinds. It is unavoidable that any law should have such an effect. The private nature of actions for libel and defamation when they do occur seems adequately to mark out restrictive features here as a special case.

It should be pointed out that the justifications of even minimalist restrictive action on libel seem to go against the common liberal argument that the best test of truth is in the market-place. However that may be, it is possible to justify action against defamation as analogous to action against physical assault; each involves harm against an individual, although in the former case of a perhaps less easily definable kind. The greater subjective element in assessing the harm done to a reputation by defamation and its material consequences may account for the private nature of action at law. The fact that non-physical harm is typically no threat to the state may also render unnecessary direct public action against it. Occasionally, of course, libel may prove to be a threat to public order, and the offence of criminal libel[3] is occasionally activated in English law.

Fraud

The restrictions on free speech connected with fraud may also be accounted for in a special way. In some cases, of course, fraud will lead (or would lead, if unchecked) to direct breach of contract or the actual commission of a crime such as theft (which would fall straightforwardly under the necessity to prevent criminal acts and the threats to society which they pose). In other cases, however, the law is concerned with the publication of fraudulent claims and attempted deception to procure otherwise legitimate advantages for the perpetrator, such as, in a trivial case, through the misrepresentation of the qualities of a product in order to sell it; then the justification of legal action against it requires a special interpretation. It may be accounted for in terms of paternalistic protection, and in societies where this kind of protection is widespread it will form an unexceptional part of a protective system. On this rationale, protection against fraud is easily associated with other measures of consumer protection. But the present discussion concerns the *necessary* limitations to freedom of speech, and while fraud seems a necessary area for action, other protective measures do not seem to rest on a similar necessity to curb free speech, and therefore they will not be helpful here in explaining why fraud must be acted against.

As a necessary limitation of free speech, action against fraud is best seen as action against false pretences, and a logically acceptable extension of action against deception of other kinds. With restrictions related to false pretences and not protection we are more readily able to distinguish fraudulent from merely exaggerated claims, and attempts at actual deception from attempts at persuasion only. Thus, once the idea of a strictly minimal interference is accepted, firm limits can be set to rightful restrictive action. But when it is felt that exaggeration is tantamount to fraud, that persuasion is as socially undesirable as deception, any limitation of interference to a minimum has been abandoned.

Public Order and Subversion

The problems of defamation and fraud are, in a way, incidental to the main problem of the limits of free speech, which is the relation of those limits to public order and the preservation of society. The desirability of restrictions in the interests of public order pure and simple is surely not seriously in dispute. A basic conception of such rightful limitation of free speech is found in Mill's example (its old-fashioned image detracts not a whit from its contemporary significance): an opinion that dealers in corn are starvers of the poor may not be expressed publicly to an excited mob outside a corn dealer's.[4] This seems a legitimate restriction even if the intention to incite violence is absent. To go beyond an example as uncomplicated as this quickly raises difficulties. May the opinion be expressed if the mob is in the next street, or if it is a mile away in some meeting-hall, or if a disturbance is feared tomorrow, or next week, caused by people in the audience addressed by the speaker? Why does it become permissible if expressed in restrained language in an intellectual journal? Physical or temporal distance often cannot be the central consideration: there are instances enough of disorderly mobs travelling more than a mile to wreak vengeance, or restraining their wrath for a day or two. There is more to the problem of what constitutes a real threat to public order and therefore provides reasonable grounds for the limitation of free speech than a literal consideration of the separation between the threat and its possible realization. The viability of a principle of separation might be re-established by pointing out that although a crowd may set out with evil intent or may bide its time till the morrow, it may be stopped before its object is fulfilled; but, of course, serious disorder may break out where or when the crowd is frustrated, and the corn dealer may be saved from violence at the expense of the police and innocent members of the public.

The consequences of incitement may be no less serious when a crowd is at a physical remove from its object; thus physical distance cannot be the real deciding factor for the imposition of restrictions. Nor has a temporal remove any overriding significance: people can be provoked to violent actions which require a waiting period before they can be realized. What we might call an 'emotional remove' cannot be a final criterion: a placid audience might be roused to fury by the right sort of speaker using cool but appropriate reminders of injustices suffered in the past. Intellectually detached debate can eventually filter through to provoke harm among ordinary people in the real world. What matters is whether a particular exercise of free speech seems likely to prove to be the *sufficient condition* of future violence or disorder. (Therefore what has been referred to as the seminar model[5]—the academic discussion in a small closed group as to whether dealers in corn starve the poor—is excluded, unless, perhaps, the participants are invited to incite a riot after they have left the seminar room!)

To talk of the concept of a sufficient condition, using it to supplant the idea of mere proximity, leads discussion naturally to a consideration of peaceful subversion. It becomes possible that if there seems a definite causal chain of events no different in principle, with consequences of apparently the same probability, it is right to impose restrictions for the preservation of public order, whether the likely disorder is five minutes or five years away. A competent authority is justified in acting against any threat to public order, and thus against any kind of subversive activity which threatens disorder, however ostensibly peaceful in itself.

Not all subversive activity is intended to bring about disorder, and very little is intended to bring about the disorderliness of a riotous mob.

Subversion may take place peacefully and not present a direct threat to public safety. It may also not present so much as an indirect threat, insofar as its aim may be to bring about radical social change, by substituting, one might say, one guardian of public order for another. This is often the case. For example, the infiltration of communist ministers into socialist governments in some countries immediately following the Second World War was subversive, but not of itself necessarily a threat to order; as witness to this may be cited the relatively peaceful takeovers of some of the states in question as the growing communist hold on power took effect.

Peaceful subversive activity with no aim of disorder is an awkward problem for freedom of speech. A censorship of expression based on the minimal liberal principle can seemingly do nothing against practitioners of peaceful subversion even on preventive principles, for the inception of a new kind of state by no means guarantees disorder to follow. Much political subversion, though not unconstitutional in itself, seeks to bring about political—and social—change contrary to the spirit and intentions of the constitution and seems objectionable for that reason. I began the chapter with a reference to Locke and liberalism, and it is appropriate to recall that this was as much Locke's concern about papists in seventeenth-century England[6] as it was the UnAmerican Activities Committee's worry over communists in the McCarthy era in twentieth-century America. The principal question which has seized the attention of many in this connection is the following: what is to be done about people who cannot be expected to follow those political and social conventions which are necessary not so much to the maintenance of public order and the basic mechanisms of any viable state as to the preservation of the essential character of our presently existing society?

There is one point to be made here with a specific bearing on the problem of free speech, and this is about the justification of preventive legislation. Locke's political argument against Roman Catholics was not that they had proved themselves untrustworthy in the past (although it must have appeared to Locke that this was the case) but that they were likely to prove themselves so in the future, for which their apparent past untrustworthiness was good practical evidence. The imposition on them of civil disabilities was not intended to punish them for past misdemeanours (even though such punishment might be justified in Locke's mind) but to forestall future threats to the English state as constituted; in a similar way it was the prevention of future trouble which justified the imposition of disabilities on atheists, for, undeterred by spiritual sanctions, they could not be relied on to keep their promises.

The Preservation of the State

The case for the prevention of peaceful political subversion takes us beyond the state as a 'night watchman' confined mainly to preserving public order to a stage where the state must be an active guardian of the political and social expression of its citizens. The absolutely minimal state, the preserver of public order, cannot act against political subversion so long as it does not believe that the success of that subversion would present a real threat to the physical peace and security of the population. There can be no justification on minimal principles if those who embody the authority of the state seek to preserve the *form* of the state's existence. The state cannot attempt to maintain itself as the minimal kind against the wishes of its citizens, however expressed, or indeed against successful action by some of its citizens if they carry the rest of the population with them.

The minimal state's preservation of itself, it might be argued, could be justified by the permissibility of restrictions imposed 'for the sake of protecting liberty', for after all it is to preserve liberty that the minimal state is set up in the first place, and it is this task which defines the boundaries of state action and makes the existence of the state preferable to there being no state at all. But it is no profound question to ask what liberty is being referred to here; certainly it is on the protection and enhancement of liberties of some kinds that many of the controls of modern states have been built, but at the expense of liberties of other kinds. One person's positive freedom is, perhaps, gained at the expense of another person's negative freedom: to talk simplistically of the protection of liberty tells us little.

When talking of the protection of freedom in a maximally free society, it might be stressed that the intention is to do no more than *protect* the freedom of all, and neither to enhance, develop, or correct it, nor to support the existence of the state or maintain the current order of society. This is to see society too individualistically. Given that people live in a society, their freedom is defined by the social order in which they live. To protect their existing freedom is *ipso facto* to seek to maintain that social order which creates and constitutes it, and this order has a content as well as a formal structure.[7] If the preservation of liberty is one of the state's functions, it seems that the preservation of the order of society, its structure and organization, as well as immediate public order, is a proper concern for any state which believes it has achieved or which intends to achieve the best or a better form of society.

If its aim is to protect liberty a state is justified in protecting and preserving that liberty which it believes itself to embody. So it is that the state is justifiably committed to self-preservation. The problem of subversion obliges us to take account of the fact that any state, however minimal its power and however apparently neutral its conception, is committed to those political and social ideals to which it constitutionally owes allegiance. Any state believing itself committed to the preservation of liberty is thereby committed to its own essential preservation. (Whether or not it is justifiably committed to opposing not only a peaceful but even a thoroughly constitutional threat to its own ideals is a matter too difficult to discuss on the present occasion, but if liberty is part of its foundation and if that conception of liberty is threatened, it would seem that it must be, although the allowable nature of its opposition is again problematic.)

Public Order and Social Order

Can the preservation of society with the ideals which go to define it as the kind of society it is be thought of as analogous to the preservation of public order? As far as measures of prevention are concerned the two cases are very different. In the first case almost everyone would agree that public disorder, breaches of the peace and similar disturbances should be prevented and not simply acted against when they occur. In the second case, where peaceful subversion is concerned, most people feel uneasy about preventive measures. This reaction is not confined to possible political subversion, which would entail an acknowledgment of the category of political offences: there is a general antipathy towards the idea of direct preventive action where, with the exclusion of acts like incitement, no 'ordinary' crime is immediately planned.

For free speech there are particular problems in the concept of subversion. The expression of a subversive opinion cannot itself strictly be called a subversive action, for words alone never overthrew any state, yet it may certainly lead to a subversive action on the part of another person. Suppression of subversive opinion is not direct action against subversion but a preventive measure against the possibility of subversion. Whenever any action is directly subversive the state is empowered to act; but this principle does not cover the suppression of subversive opinions, since these seem for the most part only indirectly subversive (as an inflammatory speech is not itself—in a direct or inherent sense—disorderly). Preventive action against subversive opinion seems to parallel the use of preventive measures to maintain law and order; and, with subversion as with disorder, simple notions of proximity do not seem to provide adequate criteria for restrictions.

With subversion the idea of an effect removed from or not immediately connected with the initial subversive act—the idea of distance—is, if not part of the actual concept, a closely allied notion. The idea of undermining denoted by subversion suggests an intended result that is neither immediate nor direct. It seems clear that it is the probability of the foreshadowed result and not proximity that justifies countermeasures for the protection of society. Justification is proportionate to the likelihood and not to the immediacy of the realization of a social threat. Elsewhere I have quoted Lord Devlin's belief that threats to society from moral subversion (among other kinds) are in a not too dissimilar way akin to the threats from physical disorder or an external enemy. If this is so, similar considerations for the protection of society are applicable to both in parallel ways.

If the notion of proximity is accepted as a starting-point for protective measures it seems right to extend it in the way suggested; otherwise it must be abandoned altogether, and then incitement as well as subversion must be given free rein. Following the abandonment of such a minimal liberal principle surely even the idea of a society worth protecting would have to be abandoned as well. With the natural extension of minimal principles to the prevention of subversion as well as disorder the state is empowered not only to impose restrictions as required to preserve public order but also to safeguard social order, that is, the continued existence of society in its current structure and organization and the ideals and future goals to which it commits itself and its citizens.

Individual and Society

A consideration of the minimal limits to free speech and their social function brings to the fore the importance of the preservation of society; this involves ideas which run contrary to the prevailing individualistic attitude towards restrictions. However, an individualistic approach is evident in a quite different area of thought from any yet considered; here an attempt is made to render censorship nugatory through psychological arguments. These claim, in one way or another, that no matter what its intentions and however irreproachable its practice, censorship is a pointless activity. It may be argued that pornography has little deleterious effect on a person's behaviour, on the basis of claims—most obvious in Freudian psychoanalytic theory—that the main paths of a person's sexual behaviour are determined early on in life by basic interactions within the family. The external stimulus of a book, magazine or videotape, for example, may encourage a person to engage in sexual behaviour, but it will be behaviour along lines to which he is already disposed. The correlation between pornography and sexual violence is simply that people with a tendency to such violence are likely to indulge in pornography. Pornography will not encourage the individual to experiment in new ways of sexual behaviour, and so it cannot be accused of being capable of corrupting him or her. If so, restrictions are pointless: an atmosphere of freedom will not corrupt the uncorrupted, and the so-called 'corrupt' person cannot have his corruption reversed through the imposition of restrictions.[8] Similar arguments against the restrictions of censorship could presumably be advanced in other areas of life. Much psychoanalytic theory suggests that a person's religious, political and aesthetic attitudes (among others) are likewise determined early in life.

I think it would be correct to say that psychological arguments of this kind leave most people unconvinced, at any rate about claims they may make to universal applicability. They fail to allow for the possibility that pornography may raise the threshold for experimentation and indulgence and shift the psychological boundaries of constraint separating the permitted from the forbidden. It may plausibly be suggested that it motivates some people who do harmful things to do them more often. And if there were a substantial minority of cases where erotic literature, for example, manifestly did change people's behaviour in either frequency or character, the arguments would cease to carry weight. After all, the point of the relevant laws is to prevent *some* people from being depraved and corrupted; restrictions are intended to protect perhaps a minority of people at risk. Psychological arguments as a guide to social action therefore cannot survive even a few exceptions to their claim that an absence of restrictions will not affect an adult's character and behaviour.

Psychological arguments are open to attack in two ways. The main attack against them must hold that they do not adequately grasp the purpose or rationale of censorship. I shall turn to this shortly; first, I wish to suggest the broad outline of an empirical attack against their claims.

An Empirical Flaw

The empirical claim favoured by a number of people is that a person's behaviour will not be significantly affected by exposure to the sort of material usually considered suitable for restriction or suppression. Such an argument can be vitiated by the consideration of other psychological tenets not unrelated to those ostensibly supporting the claim about the harmlessness of pornography. It is generally supposed that we suppress certain ideas and feelings from our consciousness, but that these remain with us below the level of awareness. Left alone they may remain there and never issue directly in public expression or physical action. But the release of material previously subject to censorship may provide the trigger that reawakens awareness and causes a person to experiment with new ways of behaviour or reveal a new side of his personality. In short, a predisposition to act in a certain way may be present in him, but it is nevertheless one which requires an appropriate stimulus for it to be actualized; temptation or suggestion has to be put in his path.

The plainest empirical lie to the psychological argument is given by advertising. Here is a technique expressly used to bring about a substantive change in a person's behaviour. Not all advertising is geared to getting people to switch from one brand of goods to another of the same kind. Some of it deliberately attempts to get people to try something new or behave in a significantly different way. Without the persuasive force of advertising it is difficult to believe that so many people would buy a particular kind of product or take up a new activity. True, people might always be *potentially* capable of certain forms of behaviour; they might always have had it latent within them, so to speak. But this is not what matters, or what should matter, from society's point of view. What advertising leads people to do is, at least, to discover in themselves a taste for certain behaviour such as they might well never have known about if advertising had not led them to discover it in themselves; and not only do they discover it, they give it real effect. (According to the story, the old western farmer who saw his first mail-order catalogue remarked that he never knew there were so many things he could do without; on the other hand, he might no longer have been so sure that he could do without some of them and have gone on to order one or two of the items just to see what they could do for him. Much advertising, of course, is intended to create a demand, and demand in turn may come to be internalized as subjective need.)

In an analogous way pornography may lead people to discover in themselves a taste for certain forms of sexual behaviour of which they would not previously have known themselves capable. Without the 'advertising' stimulus of pornography they might have remained quite ignorant of such an inclination and never have been tempted to indulge it. And there is no reason to believe that pornography, like advertising, may not be capable of creating a 'demand' in some people where demand—or at least no conscious demand—existed before.

In addition to this argument the psychologist's reasoning may be attacked in another way. Disregarding unconscious but unrealized tastes, and allowing for the moment that the psychologist is right in his claim that pornographic literature will not significantly corrupt a person either by bringing him to indulge in new ways of behaviour or even by actualizing a predisposition in him, we can still raise an objection along the following lines, which follow some of the reasons in arguments against pornography. The free publication of certain acts in the imaginary world of a book, magazine, film, video or on the internet in an uninhibited fashion may lead some people to misconceive true social attitudes towards those acts in the real world. The moral bonds that have previously constrained their behaviour may seem loosened through their exposure to uncensored material, and they may indulge their propensities for certain forms of behaviour more frequently, more openly and more offensively.

Psychological and Social Rationales

What has been said so far about psychological arguments bears on empirical matters. This approach does not need to be treated in more detail here but should rather be left to those with the experience required to study the facts carefully and see whether some of the psychologist's contentions are borne out in real life. I wish to turn to a detailed examination of what I referred to above as the main attack against psychological arguments, namely that they do not grasp adequately the purpose and rationale of censorship.

It is clear that those who employ a psychological argument believe that the main function of censorship is to prevent harmful effects on individuals, and it is on its practical success in fulfilling this function that it stands or falls as a worthwhile policy for the state to pursue. This is a superficial way of regarding censorship, which is worthy of a deeper and more compex study of its purposes. Much censorship is not concerned with the actual immediate harm that might come to individuals considered discretely. Some is, certainly, in particular with relation to the vulnerable, such as children; but we should understand that censorship can be understood more broadly and constructively if it is seen as functioning not to protect a relatively few immature, weak-willed or vulnerable individuals from psychological damage so much as both to regulate and to be an expression of social attitudes and society itself. We should not confuse the overt aims of some particular piece of legislation with the deeper rationale that permits and requires such legislation in general.

Elsewhere I have developed the thought that censorship contributes in an essential way to education, even though it does so in the negative way of shutting off unacceptable possibilities open to young persons. As it finds a place in education it is concerned to produce acceptable (not necessarily conforming) adults—people who are fit and proper members of society. It would be possible for censorship consistently to be carried on into adulthood with the same educational intentions.

But what is the present position of adult censorship? The vestiges of restrictions in our society (and many societies like it) still have as one of their functions the enforcement of prohibitions which would otherwise result from a more or less automatic and almost unconscious self-censorship, a capacity for which is created by the right educational process. The creation of such a capacity does not itself, of course, arise from the actual imposition of restrictions but is brought about by the positive moral and social education undergone by the child. The idea that education enables the child to make a 'proper choice' later in life means that he should come to reject certain alternatives that would otherwise present themselves as open to him. Active censorship restricting freedom of information for adults is a measure of the failure of this part of the educational process.

In our society it is one of the aims of education not to make the individual conform to a single approved lifestyle but to ensure that he or she adopts one among several acceptable styles. The adult's freedom of choice is characterized by the retention of certain fixed social parameters which entail that some possible lifestyles cannot be regarded as an acceptable exercise of freedom of choice. Often enough this aim is not realized in practice. Acknowledging that the educational process fails in many cases to develop proper maturity of opinion, society imposes measures to take the place of the individual's own self-censorship. It thus seeks only to do through censorship what it intended that individuals should do for themselves; it does what it would consider should ideally not need to be done.

The psychologist may agree that censorship of a public kind is intended to remedy the lack of self-censorship, but contend that in doing so it is superfluous, misguided, or even counterproductive. The individual's personality is not going to be affected one way or the other in any profound way. To answer this objection we must go on to discover why society wants individuals not to express themselves in disapproved ways or come into contact with certain types of expression, and why, therefore, psychological, individualistic arguments have no force.

If specific attention is given to the active concept of expressing oneself in contrast to the more passive one of being a reader or member of an audience for someone else's expression, we shall come closer to understanding the social rationale of censorship, for in preventing or modifying expression a society is not working merely for the prevention of access (with the purpose of individual protection) at a more fundamental stage or in a more effective way. This may be one of censorship's purposes, but it is by no means an exhaustive description of all that censorship may set out to achieve. In fine, in concerning itself with the matter of expression regarding its individual memebers, society is concerned with its own self-expression.

As it seems to imply a strong—and, for some, a bizarre—notion of the personification of society, the claim that society can be concerned with its own self-expression requires elucidation. In some monistic and homogeneous societies censorship and other apparent restrictions of liberties will not be negative and unacceptable because they have been *imposed* on the community, rather they will be positive social phenomena arising naturally out of the community and serving as an aid to its integration and development. Historically it is possible to find such features as the following in some societies: a close association, if not a complete identification, of law and morality; a close relationship of religion with morality and with all social life; not simply an intolerance of people with strange or deviant ideas but a genuine inability even to comprehend them, so that the practised intolerance is itself genuine and comprehensible; and a lack of discrimination between 'facts' and 'values', with the result that the latter appear equally as objective as the former. The most noteworthy consequence of these features is a lack of freedom, as we understand it; but this is not felt as a lack of freedom until heterogeneous social tendencies develop. In a stable, homogeneous society censorship and other restrictions of liberty are not imposed on the community by some external or authoritarian power, they arise organically from within the community itself.

In the many heterogeneous and pluralist societies existing today such ideas appear to have little applicability. These societies do not possess an organic or conceptual unity. The clearest indication of a substantive pluralism is surely the loss of a common ideal for a society: thus today not only are we not agreed about the means needed for a course of action to be effective but also, in many cases, we are not agreed on the ends we are working towards.

With the loss of common ideals censorship forfeits its strongest rationale, which is its natural role as a reinforcement of an organic structure of social values. Measures of censorship in our own society are patchy, inconsistent, often ineffective, and unco-ordinated in their justification. It is no matter for wonder, therefore, that the very idea of censorship should be questioned even in extreme cases where restrictions seem to have a *prima facie* appropriateness. Censorship is imposed fairly consistently, if too extensively, in the interests of national security. Beyond that, however, it seems that to stop the expression of ideas that are unpleasant (or worse) to some people, or to prevent other people being encouraged to think such thoughts—however meretorious its intentions may be—is a denial of simple free speech.

Almost nobody believes that free speech should not be denied in at least some of the familiar cases, but to suggest, as many who support restrictions believe, that these restrictions somehow are not really examples of censorship or violations of freedom of speech is untenable. After all, literally free speech should know no constraints at all. We may perhaps legitimately restrict free speech to prevent immediate physical or economic harm, but when censorship is employed in the interests of public morality its patchiness and the incompleteness of possible complementary measures makes its rationale appear unconvincing. New areas of censorship result from virtual *ad hoc* enactments and are, like race relations legislation, simply anomalous in their connections with the principle of free speech. It is these anomalies and the attempt to reconcile them with the principles from which they derogate which fuel the extensive political and philosophical debates on the subject.[9]

In a pluralist state there can be no provision for a reasonable theory of social censorship except, perhaps, in specific, limited areas where different constituent groups are in agreement; otherwise restrictions will typically be *imposed* on the citizens of such a state and not arise naturally out of deep social attitudes. The remnants of a censorship with consistent principles now left to us remind us that the basis of restrictions was generally a Christian conception of social and moral values. The fact that principles of restriction are in dispute is a sign not so much of a society that is becoming increasingly liberal but of one that is becoming increasingly heterogeneous. This point is to be emphasized, for liberalization is not necessarily to be correlated with a growing absence of restrictions; a free society is not a society in which there are no restrictions, for that is an impossibility, but one in which restrictions (as they seem to an external observer) are believed reasonable and acceptable, and are indeed not felt as *real* restrictions at all.

Restrictions in society can only exist acceptably where the body of people constituting that society share common interests and ideals that extend throughout their whole way of life, since in the end values canot be rigidly demarcated. Such a group will share a common conceptual life and have an agreed understanding of what their social order consists in. It is in this type of society that a so-called restriction like censorship becomes not a negative imposition of restraints but a positive way of enhancing, developing and maintaining the life of a society. It is impossible to reconcile censorship with the modern idea of a pluralist society, since an acceptable system of censorship must be based on a single substantive interpretation of common principles, and this is not found in such a society. Perhaps censorship can be applied to the extent that a few principles happen to coincide, but such a practice, through its incompleteness and lack of depth, must inevitably lose conviction. It is conviction that positive restrictions require.

The Needs of Social Order

Part of the rationale of censorship is its contribution to the maintenance of social cohesion; one of its aims therefore is the muting of dissent. One benefit claimed for society on behalf of free speech is that dissent and the discussion of competing beliefs and opinions are, as pointed out earlier, 'an aid to the intelligent and living apprehension of a truth'.[10] The familiar argument that if we silence dissent we may be silencing the truth admittedly counts against censorship. To speak out against error or falsehood is in normal circumstances a desirable thing to do. To suppress free speech, to make it unwise for people to speak out by the threat of severe penalties if they do so, and even to attempt to encourage them to exercise self-restraint therefore constitute a disservice both to knowledge and to the people concerned.

However, the argument which gives priority to the claims of truth and knowledge asserts not simply that free speech is beneficial for the individual—if that were all, it would not interest us at this point—but, more importantly, that it is beneficial for society. The presence of many intellectually healthy citizens is socially advantageous; the allowing of a diversity of individual opinions is to the general benefit of society as a whole. It is to be noted that this kind of argument remains steadfastly consequentialist and utilitarian.

One purpose of censorship is to ensure that right opinion, as accepted and defined by those in authority, is not threatened. Such right opinion will be threatened if those who criticize or speak out against it are allowed to express themselves freely, possibly achieving a wide dissemination of their ideas. The first results of the publication of heterodox ideas will be that a number of people who have until then subscribed without question to the received opinion will begin to experience doubts about it. If the general aim of censorship is to perpetuate a certain system, then its immediate aim must be to keep it secure, and hence to keep people steadfast in their beliefs and free from doubt.

Right opinion (in this sense) and truth may not coincide. In suppressing free speech in order to maintain right opinion the authorities may come to suppress the truth or some worthwhile idea. Objectors to censorship consider that this possibility provides a central reason for permitting free expression. Indirectly, of course, suppressing some dangerous truth may help to maintain right opinion. Suppressing the publication of instructions on how to manufacture and assemble terrorist explosives or produce poison gas will also suppress the expression of socially unwelcome opinion and condemn such opinion by association. In this case, many people would believe that the suppression of opinion was a worthwhile and morally acceptable price to pay to maintain their own personal safety.

Mill's belief that even bad ideas and wrong opinions have value is less commonly endorsed; but it does rule out the possibility of arguing in support of censorship from the worthlessness of many individual opinions, for it is not individual opinion with which we should be concerned, but the intellectual climate as a whole, including the system of censorship or toleration as a whole.[11] A policy of censorship operated with the best intentions will undoubtedly suppress and restrict much that, in the opinion of the majority, ought never to have seen the light of day, but in individual cases a rigorous and efficient system of censorship will also frequently suppress the truth, good ideas, useful opinions and tenable beliefs. The advocate of maximal freedom of speech may overstate or misstate his case; nevertheless, that case in substance remains. However good the intentions of the censor, the situation in practice is likely to go against them; and with successful censorship it would appear that the damage which is done can never be known.

That so much past or present discussion of censorship and free speech has been in terms of its relation to truth, progress, the life of reason, and the general intellectual climate of a society is quite to be expected. If censorship has the ulterior motive of protecting truth then its activities bear a *direct* relation to truth. Its suppression of wrong opinion is a direct suppression of supposed error, and its prohibition of informative material is a direct action against unwanted knowledge. But on the other hand, if censorship exists with the primary purpose of protecting social order its actions only intermittently relate to social order: they are carried out only to influence social conditions and to support *indirectly* the continuance of the established order. The protection of truth by restrictive activities on the authorities' part becomes no longer an end in itself but rather a means to the end of preserving the integrity of society. The ostensible purpose of restrictions will often disguise their real social function. Objections against censorship are valid to the extent that they refer to the direct results of censorship, but the preservation of social cohesion and order is quite different from the protection of truth since these can only be preserved by the indirect means of protecting and defending the knowledge and beliefs of a society in its members, its institutions and other social manifestations.[12]

Censorship and Social Order

The common idea that censorship is concerned with truth and right opinion is hardly totally wrong. Whatever the intentions of censorship, it must always have an important bearing on truth. When censorship is looked at from the point of view of the vindication of free speech rather than of the justification of restrictive policies truth will seem to be the principal consideration, but from the other point of view the argument for permitting the critic to air his views seems not to hold so clearly; as Dr Johnson remarked, 'if every murmurer against government may diffuse discontent, there can be no peace'.[13] In protecting social order censorship concerns itself also with an immediate object, that is to say, with expression. 'Social order' is manifested in what people say and do, in how they express themselves; therefore censorship shows a concern with the beliefs people express and the knowledge they have to communicate. It seeks to control the attitudes underlying social cohesion by suppressing contact with opinions of the wrong kind. Where necessary it seeks to determine ideas and opinions. But it can only act externally. While censorship, through its restriction of free access to information and free inquiry, significantly affects a person's ability to hold certain opinions and beliefs and possess certain kinds of knowledge its chief overt concern will be that opinion and information of specified types should not be expressed, or if they are expressed, that the usual consequences of expression, namely its influence on other people's thoughts and actions, should be nullified to the greatest extent possible. If someone does not hold a certain belief, how can he or she express it? But if, despite restrictive measures, that person comes to acquire it, censorship has not been defeated, for in the interests of social order it will still strive to prevent further communicative expression of that belief.

In this social function of censorship restrictive measures are in a stronger position regarding their intended efficacity. It is not logically necessary that they be so, yet censorship and other restrictive measures are typically conservative in intent: they seek to preserve not quite the status quo but certainly a real continuity in society's nature and aims, and they do not appear to question the intrinsic value of its foundations and principles. This is true even in a revolutionary situation. The leaders of a revolution may attempt to destroy knowledge about the previous regime, but they immediately seek to conserve the revolution which has just taken place.

It is natural therefore that in arguments about censorship a conception of the censor's activities as unsubtle and unadaptable often accompanies a conviction that censorship is ultimately pointless as a practice and unsuccessful. It might be that in the long term social order would not be best served by that sort of rigid censorship which appeared to conduce to it in the short term. But in such circumstances the censoring authority, not necessarily being blind to future possibilities, *could* grasp the long-term prospects and act accordingly. Censorship does not have to be unsubtle. There is no reason to suppose that in pursuit of its aims censorship need be a rigid policy, although, if it did develop a fluid approach, this might seem to less discerning people a sign of caprice on the censors' part.

Censorship can be effective as a means to some ends but not all. It can be effective in contributing towards the maintenance of some societies but not—easily—towards the advancement of truth and knowledge as such. A universal condemnation of censorship as ineffective (or counterproductive) cannot be accepted. It can be effective, and it can be founded on aims which in themselves are acceptable. Censorship as an end in itself is not justified. Certain ends which might be attained by means of censorship are justifiable. One question remains: may censorship be morally acceptable as a means to those ends?

Is Censorship Intrinsically Wrong?

Most arguments against censorship claim either that its ends are wrong or that the restrictive means chosen to attain those ends are ineffective, as well as on claims that although the ends are right, such means to those ends are inadmissible. I hope that I have shown that censorship as a means need not be ineffective, but that whether it is will depend partly on its aims. Some aims are morally acceptable and even desirable.

The argument that censorship as a means is intrinsically wrong might be based on a consideration of the restrictiveness of censorship, notably the limiting of individual free expression. This argument would require that an individual has a right not simply to free speech, but a more interesting positive right to dissent actively, to speak out whatever the consequences not just for him as a person but for society too. No right of substance, however, can be recognized to be absolute in any society which values its essential nature. There will always be some considerations which make it necessary in one or another connection that a specific right be abrogated for a period or overruled in specific cases. Were censorship to be considered intrinsically wrong, we should have to conclude that a person did have a right to literal free speech that was inalienable. Given that no right is absolute, it is necessary to determine that level of censorship and other restrictions which is compatible with and required by relevant social circumstances and the aims of society for the future. If there is a right to free speech (if we wish to retain the term), under certain conditions it may, like other freedoms of consequence, properly be curtailed or suspended. To imply that free speech is somehow no less free when it is *legitimately* curtailed is a nonsense.

What is needful is not to justify the aims of censorship, which would seem possible, but to discuss whether censorship could prove a viable means in pursuit of the ends involved. It seems that for such ends as truth, right belief, or unhampered progress in knowledge it is not, although a situation of total freedom is not as unequivocally beneficial for them as the opponents of censorship sometimes argue. But for conservatism, the furtherance of social order and the maintenance of social integrity, censorship can prove useful.

It is surely an untenable claim that when we are confronted by a choice between truth and social order we must exclusively opt for one and the same value as determining our actions on every occasion. Should truth always prevail regardless of the consequences for society, or social order be maintained even at the cost of systematic widespread lies and the deliberate deception of ordinary people by the authorities if this is the necessary means? The complexities of a real situation may be such that the choice between truth and order is a difficult one to make. What must be explicitly asserted—for it is evidently not denied in practice—is that sometimes it is right to give precedence to the claims of society and its survival over the claims of truth and personal autonomy.

The Enduring Presence of Restrictions

Restrictions in our social lives are always with us, and must be. It is hard to imagine—or rather, it is impossible to conceive—what a totally free *society* might be like, since unfettered freedom implies a reversion to a Hobbesian state of nature which is no society at all. In any case, nobody desires a society that is in the literal sense that free, even if it were possible: its absurdity becomes apparent as we try to think about it. But we can easily understand what sort of self-limitations on their behaviour and freedoms, including freedom of speech, would come naturally to reasonable people—or so we believe.

But can we really? What comes naturally in one society is a sign of oppression in another; the mark of a free person for one thinker is the mark of a slave for another. Unregulated liberty becomes characterized as licence. Hegel's conception of freedom is for some the progenitor of modern totalitarianism, while Marx could assert that freedom is the recognition of necessity. If we allow that certain limitations come naturally to reasonable people, what content do we give to our concept of the reasonable person? He or she cannot be defined simply as the person who makes the right use of individual freedom.

Restrictions are required—whether they are self-imposed or ordained by authority—because our actions are forever impinging on the lives of others. This is a commonplace. Our behaviour may affect others in many ways; but even if all other occasions for restriction are removed, it still remains the case that often when one person avails of an opportunity the opportunities of others are thereby diminished and in some cases altogether removed. Restrictions are necessary to protect the possibilities of action for others. Even with a positive duty to provide means for people to make use of their freedom, still there are limitations to be decided, if only by reference to practical necessities. From time to time there is a need to make judgments which assess the demands of parties competing for limited resources.

Of itself a refusal to publish a work for commercial or other practical reasons does not amount to censorship. Censorship, it will be remembered, is a policy of restriction, a policy which is a deliberate taking of action *against* some instance of public expression, paying attention to the object of its action, and motivated by the form or content or both of that object. In the arena of publishing (to take a traditional example) policies of marketing solely or chiefly commercial or popular material are restrictive in effect. There are only a finite number of outlets, and a commercial publisher is indispensable for worthwhile distribution; self-publishing or making use of a vanity publisher almost always is a waste of effort and money and consigns a book to oblivion. If publishers favour some kinds of material, the opportunities for other kinds will be diminished.

However, this effect is only incidental to publishers' purposes. The restrictive effects as such are not intended; they are simply a natural and inevitable consequence of a favourable attitude towards other material, and indeed a natural result of competitive features of the market. It may be argued that responsible selection should not be based on commercial considerations alone, since book publishers, like broadcasters, have a duty to respect some non-commercial criteria. Nevertheless, deliberate and positive selection is necessary for any publishing house; fiction publishers may occasionally publish an item with no eye for profit, but they still do not and are not expected to publish books on a subject like philosophy. Up to this point we can argue with some justification that no policy of censorship is in place. In general, the pursuance of a policy of selection in a situation is not tantamount to a restrictive measure. While there are plenty of other publishers around, one publisher's rejection of a manuscript does not constitute censorship.

Yet a problem may arise. The aspiring writer may complain that no publisher will take his or her book. Perhaps the book is not publishable on any genuinely commercial basis; and yet some (and not only the writer) might argue that the book should be provided with an outlet.[14] The argument that the book is not a commercial proposition may become a convenient way of censoring a work that carries an unwelcome argument. Counter-arguments to publishing (beyond the narrowly commercial) may take the line that the book is not academically respectable, that it is improperly researched, tendentious, poorly written and so on. These in turn may be opposed by the claim that such reasons only enshrine the very prejudices which are objected to. The question still remains: are there valid reasons for the *practical* limitation of free speech?

If we discussed simply the analytic question whether the consequences of a publisher's consideration of popularity and commercial viability amounts to censorship we should, I think, be missing the point only to get caught in not very profitable verbal definitions. Clearly, the use of commercial criteria in deciding what is publishable, which leads inexorably to the rejection of certain types of material, is not censorship, direct or indirect. But is it, while not strictly an infringement of free speech, nevertheless detrimental to free speech? That is to say, we ask not whether the rejection of material for apparently commercial considerations means the denial of freedom of expression to the person involved but rather (more positively) what the limits are to the necessary provisions which a society must make in order for true freedom of expression to exist.

There can be no automatic link between a general social commitment to freedom of expression and any specific indivdiual's right to publicize and disseminate his or her opinions. To say that all people have the right to express themselves freely cannot entail that they have the right to demand and be given facilities to publish their thoughts.[15] Much material for publication is quite rightly rejected not only on commercial grounds but also on grounds of style or presentation or of what might generally be termed plain inferiority of thought or expression. Material is acceptably turned down when it lacks some quality considered necessary for publication irrespective of content.

But now we can make two points in this connection. First, this reference to the assessment of quality being quite fair when work is considered for publication—that inferior work just does not get published—should carry no reference at all to the content of the work, the actual subject-matter, the opinions presented or the general 'school of thought' or world-view to which the work belongs. Second, if no account of content as such is taken, then criteria for assessment must be equivalent as between different material; the same criteria must be used in assessing material acceptable in content as are used in assessing material the content of which is *prima facie* unacceptable because of the nature of the opinions expressed. As far as providing a person with a 'real' right to freedom of expression, as provided by significant publication, no account is to be taken of the substance of the content, the opinions expressed or the general attitude conveyed, unless, that is, one is prepared to accept the opprobrium of limiting expression.

In a way the foregoing paragraphs have been something of a digression. True though it is that what is excluded falls by the wayside, rejection of a proposed publication on the ground that it fails to meet standard (non-ideological) criteria is not equivalent to censorship unless the stated reason is used to hide a deeper motivation. Arguments against censorship do not lead to an obligation to make positive provision for people to express themselves. Of course, it is true to say that the right to freedom of speech is fine but not much good if you cannot get anybody to listen to you or do not have the wherewithal to enable other people to listen to you. Nevertheless, we must be careful to distinguish between the society which forbids you the wherewithal to do so and the society which simply does not provide it. The prohibition of the use of certain channels of communication for the expression and propagation of ideas or information may amount to censorship, but of itself the lack of subsidized provision does not.

However, from the discussion above we can see that the selection process may as easily and as properly take not the positive form of selecting what is acceptable or demanded but the negative form of discarding and excluding what is unwanted or undesirable, and this discarding of unwanted material may be motivated by purposes unrelated to the apparently objective criteria cited (such as commercial viability). Is this censorship? The original definition of censorship was that it related to content subverting the governing authority or the social and moral order. The argument against censorship must not be an argument against all restrictions—a level to which it is sometimes expanded—but one against restrictions of a certain kind, with a certain purpose, imposed in a certain way and on a certain type of content. Yet I suggested in the introductory section of this book that restrictions of ostensibly different kinds were difficult to separate; various restrictions, understood in the light of their methods and purposes, often merged with each other as far as the development of a theoretical justification was concerned. Even so, I have shown that censorship of many kinds (including peripheral varieties) is still related to the original definition linking censorship to authority and order.

Social Consolidation

Can restrictions be applied in selecting material without incurring charges of censorship? Popularity is one criterion of selection and undoubtedly a weighty consideration in the provision of the means of public expression for an artist, writer or speaker. But popularity cannot be the sole criterion. This is not because a minority of people might thereby get nothing that they wanted; it is possible for everybody to get a proportion of what they want individually, if we assume, plausibly, the usual diversity of tastes in a population. Popularity cannot be the sole criterion because the responsible newspaper editor or television programmer, for example, believes that people should be offered something from time to time which they do not obviously want, or which they will realize afterwards they have enjoyed or found useful or informative although they never expected to. Responsibility thus may involve from time to time an ostensibly antidemocratic imposition of values, even though in the ideal situation intentions are to be vindicated retrospectively. Popularity has a place but it is modified by other considerations.

A responsible attitude here does not involve an intention to prevent the subversion of an existing social or moral order; but it does involve an intention to contribute in some way to the consolidation or amelioration of the existing one—or sometimes, perhaps, to the building of a new one. A simple formulation of such an intent is the argument that 'we must educate our masters'.[16] I should wish to argue that this process of selection of material for publication or broadcasting on other than straightforward principles—of provision proportionate to demand, for example—this partial imposition of taste disproportionately to apparent desires, is not entirely misdescribed when it is spoken of in terms of censorship and restrictiveness. It is not a kind of category mistake to talk of selection in this way, for it is a positive policy that is a direct counterpart of the negative policy of censorship. This statement requires some explanation before I discuss its consequences.

Censorship is a negative policy; this is self-evident, for it is a policy of restriction. Action that is its positive counterpart focuses rather on what is to be allowed, indeed, more strongly, on what is to be assisted in its public presentation. Nevertheless, in its realization this positive counterpart brings restrictions in its wake. Restrictions are not simply a *contingent* result of such a policy; to endorse a policy of positive assistance is thereby to endorse the concomitant restrictions it *necessarily* entails. The disbursement of limited public funds by Arts Councils and similar organizations, for example, raises problems. To assist some writers or artists in the expression of their ideas or the presentation of their work is, in a world with finite resources, to impair the opportunities of other writers or artists even though no decision is taken to refuse funding or other assistance directly. And since the focus of attention is not on individual persons but on types of ideas or opinions, we may say, more seriously, that to give an opportunity to one kind of idea is to take away or diminish an opportunity for another kind.

No plea in mitigation can be made that a serious charge of restrictive intent cannot be substantiated here insofar as the restrictions that come about are not deliberately visited on a specific kind of subject-matter, or in other words that although restrictions are necessitated by practicalities they only accidentally fall on some *particular* person or idea. This argument is not viable, since what is favoured goes to define whatever (indirectly) finds disfavour. Restrictions of a specific kind inevitably follow from any positive policy. The impairment of another writer's or artist's chances is therefore tantamount to a negligent, if unintentional, restriction, to which the concept of censorship is not wholly inappropriate but bears a definite relationship. Censorship is marked not only by intentions but also by results.

Results may happen by accident or through inadvertence; they may knowingly come about; they may be intended. Each kind of result shades into the next. That which happens unforeseen, when it repeatedly occurs by dint of the same policy, becomes something that knowingly comes about. That which knowingly comes about may, in suitable circumstances, become a result, not intended perhaps, but certainly expected and accepted. 'States privilege certain understandings of the community, and this inevitably disadvantages alternative understandings.'[17] Following which, welcome results may become as good as intended, if they are thought to be useful adjuncts to some policy and are readily accepted.

Obviously it is not only the most clear-cut case of intended result that is to count as censorship, for where restrictions come about as a useful by-product of a policy and are readily permitted, they are tantamount to intended restrictions. Thus there is censorship by price where an artificially high price is placed on a book to limit its sale; but again, a book may be tolerated simply because it happens to bear a high price as a genuine consequence of high production costs. Exhibitions may be seen by club members but not by the general public. Restrictions may come about by reason of a shortage of time, money, materials, resources, personnel, and many other factors. Such limitations can save the authorities the trouble of taking the decision to censor. So long as steps are not taken to correct such adverse conditions with complete indifference to the work concerned, to that extent free speech is modified and restrictions accepted for what they are and are given tacit support.

In a society with a positive commitment to freedom of speech, and therewith to affirmative rights of access to media of communication, there is a corresponding obligation to have what might be called positive intentions. It is not a matter simply of not intending restrictions, but of intending conditions which will promote the greatest freedom. It is unacceptable knowingly to allow a restrictive result when there is the possibility of averting it in some reasonable way. Accidental results require to be corrected; the results of negligence are as unacceptable in this special case as they normally are in not a few matters of law; while to make use of restrictions that happen to have come about for other reasons is surely more culpable in a moral perspective. Yet a society with a positive commitment to free speech would be required to rectify disadvantages indiscriminately.

It is this point which returns us to the main theme of this part of the book. While many people desire freedom of expression and information for themselves and others of like mind, few people would wish such freedom to be promoted indiscriminately for everyone. Restrictions are always present in society, and are required to be. The positive commitment to free speech is not a commitment to free speech for all, but a commitment to help promote certain kinds of ideas expressed in acceptable ways. We reasonably expect a balanced availability of information, but because the achievement of balance requires a process of selection that is necessarily evaluative we must accept that certain kinds of ideas will be preferred to others. For many people the class of those that will be should ideally coincide with the class of those that ought to be. This, as should have been made plain by the present discussion, means that ideas in unfavoured areas are restricted, and to a degree restricted intentionally. Given a commitment to any kind of positive promotion of favoured topics or ideas, restrictions are bound to follow.

If restrictions are a consequence of a positive policy, it would seem that the positive promotion of certain ideas and opinions could with little inexactness be expressed as the negative policy of denying or limiting opportunities for the expression of other ideas and opinions. The natural counterpart of positive stimulation and encouragement of good material is the discouragement and restriction of bad material, which can effectively be carried out through censorship and related measures. It would seem honest, at least, to make the aims of implicit restrictions clear, to set out their rationale, and to explain how they follow from a set of social presuppositions. Otherwise the situation remains one which neither commits itself fully to its own implied values nor follows the logic of complete lack of restraint through to its proper conclusion.

Censorship in Society

In my discussion of censorship in this book I have attempted to examine some of its basic motivations and purposes in relation to their theoretical aspects. This has required me to explore in part the relationship between freedom of speech and other freedoms and general values. Different social values cannot compatibly be given equal weightings, although once they have been assessed and ranked it is not necessary that they should then be unresolvably in conflict. Values do have to be assessed. If we wish to maintain the primacy of the value of free speech, then its maintenance may be at the expense of some other characteristics of our social life that we value highly. Free speech is not a solitary feature of society unrelated to all other features; it does not possess a value to be considered in a kind of conceptual vacuum. If primacy is to be accorded free speech, it must also be made clear on what grounds it can be supported and account taken of the grounds on which it can plausibly be opposed.

However strong the conceptual and moral arguments for free speech, which seem for some to make it an absolute right in principle, it can never be such in practice. The most basic needs of society demand restrictions on individual freedoms. Other-regarding actions give those who are or may be affected some rights over the agent. A problem arises when the state comes into the picture as a third party. My authority to oppose actions directed towards or affecting me substantially (circumscribed though it may be in modern societies) is surely undisputed in principle. But what is the position where individual rights of interference have apparently been delegated to the state?

A person of the classic liberal disposition is likely to say that I am free to switch off a television programme that I find offensive, or that, despite the attractions of its cover, I am never literally compelled and therefore remain free to decline to buy a book that is in bad taste. Even less can I object where to view the offensive material I have to initiate a positive action such as, for example, inserting a videotape into a machine and switching it on, or typing in a web address and clicking on a mouse. Of course, in many cases it may be that I genuinely choose to read or view offensive material. Actions may be decided by conscious choices; but that does not mean that all actions in similar circumstances are the result of deliberate decision. The ordinary person may be watching an offensive television programme without deliberately choosing to do so; he or she may buy a book because its blurb has sparked interest, without giving much thought to the real nature of its contents. People may rent a video to while away a couple of hours in the evening, genuinely misunderstanding what it was that they were getting.

In actuality the so-called free situation often presents no more of a *real* choice for a person than the restrictive situation. The opponent of censorship cannot argue that censorship *always* effectively limits people's choices or restricts thair real opportunities, on the ground that the free situation *ensures* that people will watch a programme, read what interests them or listen to arguments and discussions as a matter of definite decision. To assert this is not to adopt an objectionable elitist position. Choice frequently requires knowledge which the ordinary person cannot always be expected to have. The innocent viewer of what appears to be a quite unexceptionable programme may be caused offence before he realizes its true character. The reader of a pornographic novel may begin to be corrupted before he realizes what is happening to him, or the unwitting first step towards his own corruption may encourage him to take the second step voluntarily.

The opponent of censorship argues that restrictions limit people's freedom to choose and to act. Yet this argument only has force in social practice if people genuinely *feel* these restrictions; if it is a purely logical point that their freedom is limited (and as such it is unanswerable), it is of little practical consequence. In the real world it is surely right that the appropriate authority takes note of what actual uses people make of their potentialities and to what ends people in fact employ their freedoms. The opponent of censorship argues in terms of a world where free choices and decisions are made according to the ideal pattern, and in such a way that the claim seems to be that that ideal world, in which restrictions would not be necessary, is already here. It is evident that the way in which people actually behave when subjected to influences of one kind or another is far from the ideal. Given that the ideal is a desirable one, it is necessary surely even for the opponent of censorship to agree that people should be educated towards the ideal.

But what is to be done in the meantime? What is to be done in a situation where choice is exercised far from perfectly, and where conditions often do not favour proper choices being made or individual freedom being profitably used? If educative measures are required here, then the absence of restrictions may itself be an impediment to a proper education for freedom. Censorship may often be negative in its conception. It may be uninterested in the social benefits of a restrictive policy, in the betterment of conditions, in protection now as preparation for a future situation closer to the ideal, and be concerned only with short-term expediencies. On the other hand, its intentions in applying restrictions to adults may be linked to the general social attitudes and aims underlying the restrictions found in children's education, which should be the restrictions of a well-intentioned paternalism.

The argument for the greatest possible freedom presupposes either that people will make best use of it or that they are the best judges of their own interests and therefore nobody could choose better for them. In any case, they have been appropriately educated to make free choices. The argument for restriction of freedom holds on the contrary that although people generally may have the innate capacity to make proper use of freedom, they have not been educated correctly for that capacity to be fully realized in many cases. For what reason education is incomplete in practice is of no importance in this regard. It is of no consequence to point out, as Mill did, that society has had the opportunity to educate people properly while they were children and that if it has not done so it has only itself to blame. To say this only concedes the opponent's case: society is given authority to educate children because education is required in matters of morals and opinion as well as information and knowledge. Society sets standards to be achieved. If a person's education had failed or was incomplete in other areas, it could well seem right to extend tutelage beyond the normal termination of education. If it is society's fault that its own aims are not achieved in the time it gives itself, this is a cause for criticism and reproach, but not for the abandonment of attempts to give substantial realization to those aims.

These educational aims may be questioned, but to do that is far beyond the scope of this study. The present interest in lifelong learning suggests that the view is gaining ground that education is never complete, and for some people continuing eduction has something of the effectively obligatory about it. Censorship simply extends or prolongs the use of methods employed in pursuit of educational aims, which are by implication social aims. With the child it seeks to mould social expression, and with the adult it seeks to regulate it when the attempts to mould it have failed. If it is not permissible to regulate adult social expression, how can it be permissible to mould it in the same way at an earlier stage in the same person's life?

A Remark About Society

The argument against censorship requires a strongly individualistic philosophy which sees society as possessing little intrinsic, irreducible importance, and gives it—as a *society*—no rights over individual members. Its basic stipulation is only that the *individual* must exercise self-restraint (and then, perhaps, only if he feels it right to do so) in his dealings with other individuals.

It is impossible to set up one scheme of values as the paradigm in a pluralist society; in the context of a more homogeneous society it is easier to conceive of social behaviour governed by an allegiance to one set of evaluative standards only. It might be thought that one main function of much censorship is to prevent supposed harmful effects (as defined by the authorities) coming about for a significant number of persons through their exposure to a specific kind of material. (The focus of attention in the past has often been on sexual material; however, the point to be made is equally applicable to other material and recent attention has been directed to violent and racist items.) One function of censorship relating to morality is evident in the attention paid by the law to material that 'tends to deprave or corrupt'. This superficial function is unenlightening: the true rationale of censorship is not to be found in a concern with immediate harm to an individual. Censorship functions not to protect a number of susceptible persons but to conserve society and regulate social expression. The restrictions that society imposes through censorship are concerned with social expression and not with individual expression alone.

The idea of social expression may have its clearest illustration in a homogeneous society. However, it is still necessary to suggest how what I have said about censorship in this study can prove to be useful, although it cannot satisfactorily provide a living account of the sometimes vestigial restrictions that we are subjected to at the present time. If the best indication of significant pluralism in a society is the loss of a shared social ideal of some substance, then there can be no provision for a reasonable theory of censorship except where different constituent groups happen to agree on what are more or less isolated cases. Beyond this, restrictions in the pluralist state will be definitely *imposed* on many of its citizens and not arise naturally out of a unified conception of what their society ought to be like. In a homogeneous society that specific measure which those from a pluralist society may regard as an imposition or restriction may come about naturally as an expression of the character of that society and be accepted freely by its members as in complete accord with their own wishes.

Pluralist societies contain within themselves several systems of values, but by definition they cannot embody a single system. Thus there is at least potential, if not actual, conflict between these systems of values; this is a quite different situation from one in which there are disputes *within* one stable system, where some authoritative way of resolving disagreement is recognized. (It is, perhaps, rejection of the authoritative way of settling points at issue which makes the dispute one *about* systems rather than one *within* a system.) A society is more than the economic and administrative structure of the state, and to have meaning it requires shared values. It is when whole systems of values are in dispute, when many evaluative concepts central to social life become essentially contested,[18] when principles themselves rather than their occasional application merely are in question, that talk of 'one society' seems to be making use of a concept that is either doubtful or vague if anything more than rhetorical special pleading is intended. Although this may be no more than a verbal dispute in one sense, there seems to be an arguable case that at a certain point in disputes about values between two groups in the one state, we may no longer speak of one society, or even a 'divided society', but should refer to two societies or communities, who perhaps share the same external, physical lives, but do little more than that. (A similar equivocation is evident in the word 'nation', but it is not a self-contradiction to talk of a multinational state; and there would seem to be equal sense in talking of different societies or communities coexisting within one administrative structure.) As Bertrand de Jouvenel has said:

> Even as people belong to the same culture by the use of the same language, so they belong to the same society by the understanding of the same moral language. As this common moral language extends, so does society; as it breaks up, so does society.[19]

It cannot be part of the present study to attempt a complete analysis of the concept of a society or to define stupulatively the proper use of the word 'society'. It needs to be mentioned, nevertheless, that just because a population shares a geographical area and an economic, political and administrative structure, we are not entitled to claim for those reasons alone that in its entirety it constitutes, or ought to constitute, one single moral community in a deep sense or that the limited constraints acceptable in that kind of state are right for every kind of society.

With the increasingly pluralistic tendencies evident in many societies like our own we have come to revise our concept of a society so extensively that, although connected with an earlier concept which suggests a group knit together by more than material ties (a concept still prevalent in many sociological studies), it is no longer to be regarded in a meaningful sense as the same concept. Whatever word we may choose to make use of—and the word 'community', which might have been suitable here, seems increasingly devalued along similar lines[20]—there is need for a term that unequivocally refers to a body of people with common interests and ideals extending not simply to a few, often 'external', areas of their existence but throughout their whole way of life and particularly the cultural and spiritual aspects of that way of life. In sum, we should reserve a word for a body of people who are in substantive agreement about shared concepts and values.

Censorship based on shared principles, agreed to by all in their interpretation and realization, is acceptable; but this community of values is not present in a pluralist society. In a homogeneous society censorship becomes a way of regulating and directing social life in the interests of all, and, most importantly, of maintaining and intensifying the integrity of society. Our final judgment about the rightfulness of censorship and other significant restrictions on free speech must depend on our beliefs about the proper closeness of the ties which bind together the individual members of one society. The legitimacy of a set of restrictions like censorship requires that, in whatever way, the restrictions are set by society and are not simply maintained by some people who possess power to control others who lack it, for individuals have no moral right, alone or in concert, to set their ideas, beliefs or opinions as norms to be imposed on others. The liberal tradition which originates in its modern form with Mill rightly accepts this but, confined by its adherence to individualism, fails to recognize altogether the claims of society on the adult.

Notes

1 *Cf.* John Locke, *A Letter on Toleration*, translated by J.W. Gough (Oxford, 1968), pp. 130-135.

2 McCloskey, *art. cit.*, p. 221. For the record, McCloskey believes that this formulation of the principle must be rejected as unsatisfactory in practice. Rawls's treatment of liberty in general and freedom of speech in particular suggests much the same conclusion, except that Rawls's freedom of speech is decidedly political in character; see *A Theory of Justice*, pp. 222–226.

3 Strictly, the prosecution has to show that the libel has the tendency to provoke the person defamed to commit a breach of the peace.

4 Mill, *op. cit.*, p. 119.

5 The model is Alan Haworth's; see his *Free Speech* (London, 1998), p. 27.

6 *Cf.* Locke, *op. cit.*, pp. 132–135.

7 This is a political weakness (if not a moral one) in Rawls's 'thin theory of the good' as developed in *A Theory of Justice*.

8 Nevertheless, the House of Lords has effectively decided that a person can be re-depraved and re-corrupted: see *DPP* v. *Whyte* [1972] AC 849 at 863.

9 It can be argued that free speech in an ideologically neutral sense cannot exist, because it is conceptually impossible. Stanley Fish points out that 'free speech in and of itself cannot be a value and is only worth worrying about if it is in the service of something with which it cannot be identical' (*There's No Such Thing as Free Speech* (New York, 1994), p. 109). Concomitantly, therefore, we cannot 'fashion a forum in which ideas can be considered independently of political and ideological constraint' (*ibid.*, p. 115).

10 Mill, *op. cit.*, p. 106.

11 There is an intended analogy to Rawls's 'system of basic liberties' here: see *A Theory of Justice*, pp. 203–205.

12 The essence of society is not something apart from those social features of which we are, or are able to become, aware.

13 Samuel Johnson, *Works of the Most Eminent English Poets*, quoted in Donald Thomas, *A Long Time Burning* (London, 1969), p. 34.

14 I should acknowledge here that in the past and still today, despite the growth of publishing conglomerates, some publishers have been responsible for giving the reading public a substantial number of books that can never do better than break even, while many (and some not unexpectedly) do much worse. But from the point of view of free expression this makes the situation worse rather than better, since it means that publishers are exercising restrictive discrimination in choosing the lucky writers. At least a purely commercial policy has, without intending it, the virtue of intellectual impartiality.

15 We should recall Hohfeld's distinction between rights and privileges; see his *Fundamental Legal Conceptions* (New Haven, 1964), pp. 36–50.

16 This well-known adage is actually a paraphrase of the words of Robert Lowe, Viscount Sherbrooke: 'I believe it will be absolutely necessary that you should prevail on our future masters to learn their letters.' (Speech on the passing of the Reform Bill, Hansard, 15 July 1867, col. 1.)

17 Sanford Levinson, 'The Tutelary State: "Censorship," "Silencing," and the "Practices of Cultural Regulation"', in Robert C. Post (ed.), *op. cit.*, p. 199.
18 See W.B. Gallie, 'Essentially contested concepts', *Proceedings of the Aristotelian Society*, 56 (1955-56), pp. 167-198.
19 *Sovereignty*, translated by J.F. Huntington (Cambridge, 1957), p. 304.
20 It reaches its *reductio* in the term 'international community'.

Bibliography

(This is a brief bibliography intended to present only a selection of books and articles which relate directly to the themes treated in this book.)

Adams, Michael (1968): *Censorship: the Irish Experience*, Dublin: Scepter Books.

Barendt, Eric (1987): *Freedom of Speech*, Oxford: Clarendon Press.

Barron, Jerome A. (1973): *Freedom of the Press for Whom?* Bloomington: Indiana University Press.

Benenson, Peter (1961): *A Free Press*, London: Fabian Society.

Berger, Melvin (1982): *Censorship*, New York: Watts.

Berlin, Isaiah (1969): *Four Essays on Liberty*, Oxford: Oxford University Press.

Copp, David and Wendell, Susan (eds.) (1983): *Pornography and Censorship*, Buffalo, NY: Prometheus Books.

Devlin, Patrick (1965): *The Enforcement of Morals*, London: Oxford University Press.

Dhavan, Rajeev and Davies, Christie (eds.) (1978): *Censorship and Obscenity*, London: Martin Robertson.

Ernst, M.L. and Schwartz, A.U. (1964): *Censorship: the Search for the Obscene*, New York: Macmillan.

Finberg, H.P.R. (1964): 'Censorship', in de la Bedoyere, Michael (ed.), *Objections to Roman Catholicism*, London: Constable.

Fish, Stanley (1994): *There's No Such Thing as Free Speech*, New York: Oxford University Press.

Fiss, Owen M. (1996): *The Irony of Free Speech*, Cambridge, MA: Harvard University Press.

Hart, H.L.A. (1963): *Law, Liberty and Morality*, London: Oxford University Press.

Haworth, Alan (1998): *Free Speech*, London: Routledge.

Hohenberg, John (1971): *Free Press, Free People*, New York: Free Press.

Holbrook, David (ed.) (1972): *The Case Against Pornography*, London: Tom Stacey.

Hook, Sidney (1967): *The Paradoxes of Freedom*, Berkeley, CA: University of California Press.

Hunnings, Neville March (1967): *Film Censors and the Law*, London: Allen and Unwin.

Hyland, Paul and Sammells, Neil (eds.) (1992): *Writing and Censorship in Britain*, London: Routledge.

Jansen, Sue Curry (1988): *Censorship: The Knot That Binds Power and Knowledge*, New York: Oxford University Press.

King, Preston (1976): *Toleration*, London: Allen and Unwin.

Lee, Simon (1990): *The Cost of Free Speech*, London: Faber and Faber.

MacMillan, P.R. (1983): *Censorship and Public Morality*, Aldershot: Gower.

McCloskey, H.J. (1971): 'Liberty of Expression: Its Grounds and Limits (I)', *Inquiry*, 13, pp. 219–237.

Miller, J. (1972): *Censorship and the Limits of Permission*, London: Oxford University Press.

Monro, D.H. (1971): 'Liberty of Expression: Its Grounds and Limits (II)', *Inquiry*, 13, pp. 238–253.

Moon, Eric (ed.) (1969): *Book Selection and Censorship in the Sixties*, New York: Bowker.

Norris, Stephen (1976): 'Being Free to Speak and Speaking Freely' in Honderich, Ted (ed.): *Social Ends and Political Means*, London: Routledge.

O'Higgins, Paul (1972): *Censorship in Britain*, London: Nelson.

Post, Robert C. (ed.) (1998): *Censorship and Silencing: Practices of Cultural Regulation*, Los Angeles: Getty Research Institute for the History of Art and the Humanities.

Radcliffe, C.J.R. (1961): *Censors*, Cambridge: Cambridge University Press.

Scanlon, Thomas (1972): 'A theory of freedom of expression', *Philosophy and Public Affairs*, 1, pp. 204–226.

Schauer, Frederick (1982): *Free Speech: a Philosophical Enquiry*, Cambridge: Cambridge University Press.

Smolla, Rodney A. (1992): *Free Speech in an Open Society*, New York: Knopf.

Straker, J. (ed.) (1966): *Censorship in the Arts*, London: Academy of Visual Arts.

Street, Harry (1982): *Freedom, the Individual and the Law*, 5th edn., Harmondsworth: Penguin Books.

Thomas, Donald (1969): *A Long Time Burning*, London: Routledge.

Tribe, David (1973): *Questions of Censorship*, London: Allen and Unwin.

Webster, Richard (1990): *A Brief History of Blasphemy: Liberalism, Censorship and 'The Satanic Verses'*, Southwold, Suffolk: Orwell Press.

Index

For Product Safety Concerns and Information please contact our EU
representative GPSR@taylorandfrancis.com
Taylor & Francis Verlag GmbH, Kaufingerstraße 24, 80331 München, Germany

www.ingramcontent.com/pod-product-compliance
Lightning Source LLC
LaVergne TN
LVHW021726021026
849161LV00004BA/737
* 9 7 8 1 1 3 8 7 3 4 7 8 4 *